The Martha's Vineyard
Table

The Martha's Vineyard Table

by Jessica B. Harris

PHOTOGRAPHS BY SUSIE CUSHNER

CHRONICLE BOOKS
SAN FRANCISCO

Library of Congress Cataloging-in-Publication Data available.

ISBN-10: 0-8118-4999-6
ISBN-13: 978-0-8118-4999-9

Manufactured in China.

Designed by Empire Design Studio

Photographer's Acknowledgments:
The shining lights that created the essential flow for this project were my
tried-and-true friends, Helen Crowther and Jee Levin, who pulled it all
together through torrential downpours; David and Amy, for their incredible
assistance; and Fan and Don Ogilvie, who opened their arms and homes to
us with unconditional generosity. Also the children and spouses—Jenna, Kayla,
Enzo, Satchel, Owen, Benoit, Randy, and Sebastian (newly ever-present!)—
who persevered and supported our effort.

Distributed in Canada by
Raincoast Books
9050 Shaughnessy Street
Vancouver, British Columbia V6P 6E5

10 9 8 7 6 5 4 3 2 1

Chronicle Books LLC
680 Second Street
San Francisco, California 94107

www.chroniclebooks.com

Contents

Up-Island and Down-Island

For years my left wrist was decorated with

five bracelets made from beads of purple shell. Folks recognized them as far afield as San Francisco, New Orleans, and Paris, for the wampum bracelets marked me as a Vineyarder. Being accepted as a Vineyarder is being granted entrance into a special society. Vacationing on the island every summer gains you access to only a part of it; all summer visitors are not Vineyarders in the same way that all tourists are not travelers. Being one means knowing how to get things done on the island and knowing the history behind names like Amaral, Flanders, Denniston, Pacheco, Leonard, de Bettencourt, and Lippman. It means knowing where to find the best bread and the best mussels for the picking. It means remembering Darling's Candy Store when it was in the middle of Circuit Avenue, Munro's Boston House, and Wamsley's Bakery, and having a family recipe in the first edition of *The Cottagers' Cookbook*. It is knowing to take your own bottle of wine to any restaurant outside of Oak Bluffs and Edgartown and to keep your source for summer pies secret. It is growing your own tomatoes and lavender and knowing islanders who will bring you their surplus catch all seasoned up and ready to cook. It is a status granted by years of meals shared with friends on fancy linens and on bare wood planks.

My Vineyarder status comes from half a century of vacationing in the same house on the island. But the story of my connection to Martha's Vineyard goes back almost a century, to a one-room wooden schoolhouse in rural Tennessee. There, in the 1920s, my father sat and listened with saucer-wide eyes as his teacher regaled the class with tales of her vacation spent on the magical island. He never forgot her stories, and when, some thirty years later, he saw a small

advertisement for a house in Oak Bluffs on Martha's Vineyard in the back pages of the *New York Times,* he couldn't resist.

The following summer we packed the gray Studebaker and headed north via the Boston Post Road and the nascent Connecticut Turnpike to Woods Hole. There we boarded a ferry called the *Islander* and made the first of what would become our annual summer journeys. The house, a ramshackle gingerbread cottage facing the town's red clay tennis courts, was still available, and after much negotiating, my parents purchased it for the princely sum of four thousand dollars.

We were among the first of a new group of black Americans to move to the center of town. Those who had longer ties to the island remained in the Highlands—the hills behind East Chop—but others, like us, joined them and, in the intervening half-century, transformed Oak Bluffs into a town known internationally as one of the country's few traditionally black vacation spots. We had all come to be a part of Martha's Vineyard Island.

Martha's Vineyard, the larger of the two islands off the coast of Cape Cod (Nantucket is the other island), has also changed in those fifty years. It's gone from being a small resort for old-line WASPs and artsy types from the East

Coast to a summer fantasy for many Americans. The island has loomed large in the national consciousness for decades. Triumph and tragedy mix in a potpourri of famous names. Generations of Kennedys have frolicked here. The Clintons retreated here after the Lewinsky affair. John Belushi is buried here, and Carly Simon—along with numerous luminaries in the worlds of journalism, literature, music, theater, and the visual arts—maintains a house here. A plane ride can seat you next to Mike Wallace or a schoolteacher from New York City or Boston heading to his summer home. The island is a magnificent mixture of the famous and the ordinary, the bright lights of headlines and the back corridors of power. It would seem that the Vineyard has always been destined for fame. Since 1602, when Bartholomew Gosnold set foot on the sandy shores and named the island for one of his daughters, Martha's Vineyard has been a part of American history.

Over the centuries, cultures have mixed as well. First there were the Wampanoag Indians, then Portuguese from Portugal and from the Cape Verde Islands, African Americans from all over, good solid Yankees whose wrinkled faces are mapped by the sea, flashy vacationers whose names always appear in boldface in the gossip columns, Jamaicans, Brazilians, eastern Europeans, and more. All of them brought their culture and their food, making the island perfect for both vacationing and eating.

The Vineyard offers not only the clambakes and the cod, lobsters, and corn of Cape Cod and Nantucket—rivals for the affections of vacationers—but also the varied cuisines of all who have landed there. Breakfast may include French toast made from Portuguese sweet bread, a wonderful challah-like egg bread, while dinner may feature down-home barbecued ribs prepared with the Vineyard's local barbecue sauce. Indian corn puddings testify to the Native American presence on the island for thousands of years. New arrivals like the Brazilians, who do much of the maintenance work around the island, and the eastern Europeans, who drive the summer buses, have introduced foods to the mix, and now passionfruit juice, hearts of palm, and buckwheat groats share shelf space with Boston baked beans at local grocery stores.

Trying to capture the Vineyard is like trying to pick up water. Each person's Vineyard is different; it is like the elephant that the blind men "saw." Depending on the part of the island that is home and your family, habits, and desires, the vision is distinct. Whether up-island among Chilmark's rolling moors or on a shaded West Tisbury lane, or down-island in patrician Edgartown or in a rocker on a gingerbread-fringed Oak Bluffs porch, the landscape and the cast of characters change. My island is a mix of flash and familiarity, of famous names and of steadfast friends whom I have had for more than half a century. It is filled with a heavy dose of nostalgia for the quieter, homier times of my youth and an anticipatory delight in the island's future pathways. Most of all, like the pages of an overflowing scrapbook, it is filled with memories of my family and friends: each leaf is its own souvenir brimming with thoughts of laughter, of meals shared, of friends made, and of wonderful, wonderful food.

Appetizers and Porch Food

18
Smoked Bluefish Spread

19
Mommy's Deviled Ham Spread

Vineyard Haven

The last bits of frankfurter roll have been thrown to the scavenging seagulls. The announcement has been made and the thrumming of the engine has stopped. The bump indicates that you've reached the dock and the steamship folks are doing their waving dance, getting the tightly packed vehicles rapidly off the ferry. Welcome to the community of Vineyard Haven in the town of Tisbury, the island's "capital" and the point of entry for most people.

Known in the seventeenth century as Holmes Hole, the bustling down-island spot usually doesn't get so much as a nod from most travelers bound for their homes or hotels, but sooner or later many will return to pick up groceries at Cronig's, have brunch at Zephrus, or wander down Main Street and buy a book at Bunch of Grapes. The cognoscenti will make a hamburger at Woodland Variety & Grill their mission, while those in search of a more refined ambience will enjoy the water views at Tropical, or the street scene outside the window of Café Moxie.

Vineyard Haven is also home of The Black Dog Tavern, a local eatery whose black Labrador–logo items have become, for many, totemic symbols of the island. The tavern has been around since 1971, an amazing feat in a place where restaurants come and go with the frequency of summer visitors. As such, it has become the stuff of many an island culinary dream. An off-season meal at a table by the fireplace in the main dining room means winter to most residents. Long-term summer folks and day-trippers alike wait in line to sit by the sea and savor one of the kitchen's special chowders. Although the original mascot went to canine heaven long ago, a local black Labrador is almost always snoozing peacefully nearby, or posing obligingly for photos that are more treasured as souvenirs than the ubiquitous T-shirts.

Smoked Bluefish Spread

3 ounces smoked bluefish
(see Sources, page 198),
flaked and then shredded

1 cup whipped cream cheese

1½ teaspoons prepared
horseradish

½ teaspoon freshly squeezed
lemon juice

Dash of pepper vinegar (see
Vinegared Chiles, page 75)

Dash of Worcestershire
sauce, or to taste

Salt and freshly ground black
pepper to taste

Bluefish is an oily fish and not to everyone's liking.

Smoked bluefish, however, is another matter. It is virtually an island staple and many
people smoke their own. It is usually served as a pâté or a spread at the beginning of many
island events. There are as many versions of this spread as there are island cooks. Try this
one first, which is pretty standard, and then try adding minced yellow onion or scallion,
other seasonings, and more to make your own distinctive version. Serve with crackers.

Combine all of the ingredients in a small bowl and mix well. Cover with plastic wrap and chill for
1 hour before serving.

Mommy's Deviled Ham Spread

MAKES ABOUT 1 CUP

My mother was a member of a local Oak Bluffs club

called The Cottagers. Founded in 1956 by women from families who came to the Vineyard to summer, the still-active group has an array of summer events and gives thousands of dollars annually to various island charities. In 1977, The Cottagers published a cookbook of members' favorite recipes. My mother was a member from the early 1960s until her death in 2000, and the names on the book's pages bring the faces of my childhood to mind. I can still recall members like Delilah Pierce, who drew the cover artwork; Lurline Purvis, a friend from Brooklyn; Winnie Cumberbatch, who went to our church in New York; Connie Coveny, whose daughter was a playmate; and Helene Wareham, whom I still see from time to time during the summer holidays. The recipes tell of the Southern roots of many of the members and include items like green bean casserole and cheese grits. One of my favorites then and now is my mother's recipe for a spicy deviled ham. It is a perfect way to use the last bits of the ham that has done yeoman's duty on many a summer table. It is as good as it is simple. Serve it on crackers or toast points.

Combine all of the ingredients in a small bowl and mix well. Use only enough of the mayonnaise to bind the ham together for spreading. Cover with plastic wrap and place in the refrigerator overnight to allow the flavors to blend. Serve chilled or at room temperature.

INGREDIENTS

1 cup ground cooked ham

1 teaspoon cayenne pepper, or to taste

About 2 tablespoons mayonnaise, freshly made or Hellmann's

Guacamole

INGREDIENTS

3 small, firm but ripe Hass avocados, halved, pitted, peeled, and coarsely chopped

1 small red bell pepper, seeded and minced

1 tomato, peeled, seeded, and minced

3 scallions, including 2 inches of green tops, minced

2 teaspoons minced garlic, or to taste

1 teaspoon minced jalapeño chile, or to taste

1 tablespoon minced cilantro, or to taste (optional)

2 teaspoons freshly squeezed lime juice

1 teaspoon chili powder

Salt and freshly ground black pepper to taste

Here is another of those dishes that can turn up just about anywhere, but that work well in the summer when friends sit around and need something to nibble on. This version is a bit spicier than the usual, and is wonderful for beach picnics, boat outings, porch sitting, or whenever folks who enjoy a piquant kick in their guacamole gather. Cilantro is a love-it-or-hate-it ingredient and can be left out. The guacamole won't be the same, but you'll love it anyway. Serve with tortilla chips.

Combine all of the ingredients in a bowl and mix well. Serve immediately.

Cocktail Almonds

SERVES 6 TO 8

Sundown drinks on the front porch are a way of life

at our house in Oak Bluffs. Friends drop by knowing that there will always be a chilled bottle of something bubbly, red wine, rum, and other tipples along with something to nibble on. I like to have a couple of snacks that are ready to go in a few minutes. One item that is always in my summer larder is almonds. If I know that I've got guests coming, I'll pop them into some boiling water, peel them, and then sauté them in oil and sprinkle them with a bit of salt. Warm from the skillet, they're perfect with just about anything and make me think of the south of Spain, where they are paired with chilled sherry and anchovy-stuffed olives.

INGREDIENTS

1 pound whole natural almonds

2 tablespoons olive oil

Salt to taste

Blanch the almonds by plunging them into a pot of boiling water and leaving them for 2 minutes. Then remove from the heat, drain, and gently slip off the skins with your fingers. Pat the almonds dry.

Heat 1 tablespoon of the olive oil in a heavy skillet over medium heat. Add half of the almonds and toast them, stirring them occasionally as they brown, for 5 to 7 minutes, or until they are all a warm, even brown. Transfer the almonds to paper towels to drain. Repeat with the remaining almonds and 1 tablespoon oil.

Place the warm almonds in a brown paper bag and add salt to taste. Shake the bag to coat the almonds with the salt. Serve the nuts warm.

NOTE: You may add other seasonings, such as a pinch of ground chipotle chile or *pimentón* (smoked Spanish paprika).

{ FERRY FOOD }

The first ferry left around six o'clock each morning, and part of the fun of the initial summer trip up to Oak Bluffs was waiting with the long line of cars to see who was heading over to the island, what car they were driving that year, and who was with them. A reservation for the Studebaker always kept us out of the standby line, but Daddy liked night driving and wanted to be sure that we arrived at the ferry on time, so we were usually in the first ranks of cars.

I'd wipe the sleep from my eyes and awaken to find seagulls swooping over the lines of cars, trying to cadge scraps of food from the shoeboxes that the travelers had packed in preparation for their journey. Old habits die hard, and the vicissitudes of travel in the segregated South meant that even in the North, black families in the 1950s would no more think of hitting the road without a shoebox full of fried chicken, deviled eggs, pound cake, oranges, raisins, and a thermos full of lemonade than they would leave home without maps and a full gas tank. We would joke that if we lost our way to the Vineyard, we could simply follow the trail of chicken bones and find the ferry pier.

My mother would then hustle me into the ladies' room at the ferry stop, cover the seat with toilet paper, and complete my brief toilette so that I'd be ready to greet anyone we met.

Once on board, we'd park our car below-decks and head up to the galley for the first official tastes of summer. Simple food was served—a few hot soups, frankfurters on New England rolls, and warming drinks—but it was like a sip from the Holy Grail after long hours in the car. Words cannot describe the heady taste of oyster crackers crumbled into a paper cup of hot chowder, or of the first bite into a steamed frank on a toasted bun with relish and onions, all savored over the relentless thrum and chug of the *Islander*'s motors.

In retrospect, with a critical eye and an expanded waistline from years of food criticism, I realize that the specialness was not in the food, but rather in the circumstances. Ferry food was and is the symbolic sacrament of return to a place of peace and communion with family. With each sip and bite of ferry food, bounds are slipped on the journey from mainland to island, and cares are loosened in a return to a place that was (and occasionally still is) a sanctuary.

Spicy Edamame

1 pound frozen edamame
(soybeans in the pod)

1 jar (10½ ounces)
Indian hot mango pickle

Edamame are the green soybeans served in their pods in Japanese restaurants. The slightly slippery texture of the beans and the way they are sucked from the pod remind Southerners of boiled peanuts. They're a quick appetizer and will keep in the freezer for a summer with no problem. You can bring them from home, but you can also find them in the frozen-food section of some island supermarkets.

Place the edamame in a 5-quart saucepan with water to cover and bring to a boil over medium heat. Lower the heat and simmer for 2 minutes. Meanwhile, place the mango pickle in a blender and pulse until you have a thick sauce.

When the edamame are ready, drain them and place in a serving bowl. Pour the mango pickle sauce over the edamame and serve immediately. Remind your guests that they have to suck the soybeans from their pods, and have a bowl ready for the discarded pods.

Spicy Cashews

Ever since I first saw cashew fruits growing in the

Caribbean, and realized that there's only one little question mark of a nut hanging at the tip of each fruit, I've understood why the slightly sweet nuts are so expensive. They're another addition to my porch-party repertoire. I season them up with a dash of chili powder, the kind that is ground chile with a hint of cumin and sometimes other herbs and spices.

Melt the butter in a heavy skillet over medium heat. Add the cashews and toast them, stirring them occasionally as they brown, for 5 to 7 minutes, or until they are all lightly browned. Transfer the nuts to paper towels to drain.

Place the warm cashews in a brown paper bag and add the salt and chili powder. Shake the bag to coat the nuts with the seasonings. Serve the cashews warm.

INGREDIENTS

1½ tablespoons butter

2 cups cashew nuts

1 teaspoon salt, or to taste

2 teaspoons chili powder

Codfish
Fritters

½ pound salt cod

Vegetable oil for frying

2 small scallions, including
2 inches of green tops, minced

1 jalapeño chile, seeded and
minced, or to taste

1 small tomato, peeled,
seeded, and minced

2 cups flour

2 teaspoons baking powder

About ¾ cup water

Your favorite hot sauce
for serving

On Martha's Vineyard, we don't need Mark Kurlansky's first-rate book on cod to tell us that cod is the staff of life. It is the totemic fish in this area of the country, where it turns up as salt cod, called *bacalhau* by the Portuguese; as fresh cod; and as the baby cod known in these parts as scrod. A lean, delicately flavored fish with flaky white flesh, cod in its dried form was a standby for sailors and a mainstay of the slave trade. In that state, it journeyed to many parts of the hemisphere, including Jamaica. There it is used to make the chewy fritters known as stamp-and-go.

The fritters are not the soft, doughy *bacalaitos* of Portuguese tradition, but rather a consistent ball of dough, with a light flavoring of cod, a bit of heat, and a crunchy crust. This version is milder than the Jamaican one, but can be heated up to Caribbean hot, hot, hot with the exchange of a habanero for the jalapeño. These fritters, like other Jamaican foods, came to the Vineyard with the Jamaicans and were quickly recognized as kin to the codfish fritters traditionally served in New England.

Place the salt cod in a bowl with cold water to cover and soak overnight in the refrigerator. Drain and place in a saucepan with fresh cold water to cover. Bring to a boil over medium heat, lower the heat to a simmer, and cook for 15 minutes, or until the fish is tender. Drain the cod, let cool, and then break up into small flakes, discarding any skin and bones.

Pour the oil to a depth of about 4 inches into a heavy saucepan or Dutch oven and heat to 375°F on a deep-frying thermometer. While the oil is heating, place the flaked fish, scallions, chile, tomato, flour, and baking powder in a large bowl. Add just enough of the water to make a thick, sticky batter. Stir to mix well.

When the oil is ready, drop the batter by the teaspoonful into the hot oil, taking care not to crowd the pan. Fry, turning once, for 3 to 5 minutes, or until golden. Using a slotted spoon, transfer to paper towels to drain. Repeat with the remaining batter. Keep each batch hot in a low oven until all the fritters are cooked, then serve immediately with the hot sauce. The fritters must be eaten hot. When they cool, they turn as leaden as cannonballs.

{ PORCHES }

Up-island natives have decks with sunset views of windswept moors and sheep meadows. Those of us who live in the more urban areas of down-island may have to crane our necks (or take a walk or even ride) to see the sea. What we have, though, are porches.

Our front porches become our summer living rooms. Whether adorned with curlicues of wooden gingerbread, hanging pots of pink geraniums and purple fuchsias, or simple frames with house numbers, they are the heartbeat of our lives. In Oak Bluffs, they make some of us think of our ancestral Southern climes, as we sit in our rockers and wave to friends driving by. The pace is languid enough that some folks even slow down or pull over for a quick chat and catch-up.

The day is calibrated with the happenings on the front porch. Morning brings the first cup of coffee and the news of the day, whether found in the *Vineyard Gazette*, the *Martha's Vineyard Times*, or the *New York Times*, or even brought by the next-door neighbor. Lunch may prompt a small nap before the beach or even an alfresco meal. Preprandial conversation and perhaps a cocktail or two are the evening's happenings, followed by a nightcap and, on some nights, a wicked after-dinner cigar.

My front porch is for the public. It is here that I think of the generations of my family that have enjoyed relaxing in the rockers. I can remember my paternal grandmother's delight in discovering just how Southern the area of Oak Bluffs was in the 1950s, when everyone knew one another and a wave wasn't good enough if a short visit could be arranged. I think of my uncles and aunts and their visits, and of my cousin and her children, and most recently of sitting with my gentleman friend and watching as his granddaughter frolicked in the park across the street.

Facing the tennis courts provides my house with a daylong screen for activity, as the players volley and lob and greet one another with the delight that comes from long familiarity. Picnic tables have recently been added, so there's also the sound of families conversing over food.

My house also has a side deck. It is where I sneak away to sit and chop carrots under the wisteria arbor, or just sit back with my feet up and enjoy watching folks stroll by. This deck was my mother's creation, and it is there that I most often think of her. With a door to the kitchen, it's the perfect spot to sneak out for a rest while lunch or dinner finishes cooking, and I have created a small herb garden that

is only a step farther, a handy way station in the direction of the kitchen. This is also where I keep the grill that is the mainstay of much of my summer cooking. The deck is too small for more than two for dinner, but it makes a great supplemental kitchen and lets me prolong my summer days well into the evening.

Marinated Olives

1 can (16 ounces) pitted colossal black olives

1 tablespoon dried Greek oregano

1 teaspoon finely minced Thai chile, or to taste

2 tablespoons olive oil

Long, lazy afternoons of porch-sitting and reading

are some of the pleasures of my summers on Martha's Vineyard, but they do require nibbles. These olives are great porch food. They're easy to prepare, will keep in the fridge for a few days, and can always be available if friends should drop in. They're also a great way to make ordinary, readily available black olives special. I like to use the pitted colossal ones.

Prick each olive several times with the tip of a knife. Place the olives and all of the remaining ingredients in a bowl and mix well. Cover with plastic wrap and refrigerate for at least 3 hours to allow the flavors to blend.

Serve the olives chilled. They will keep in the refrigerator for about 2 weeks—though they're sure to be eaten long before then.

Deviled Eggs

To some they're Southern; to me they're summer.

I can remember back in the days when the trip to the Vineyard was twice the length that it is now. Then, heading north involved being taken, groggy, from my bed and ensconced in the backseat of the car, which had been prepared as a nook for me, complete with blankets and games and books. By dawn, it was time for car food, which meant deviled eggs. The yellow would always smear on the waxed paper, and I would eat it off before my mother handed me the premoistened washcloth so I could clean myself up. Later, when I located a triangular deviled-egg plate at an antique shop on the island, I damned the cholesterol naysayers and proudly served my deviled eggs on the bright yellow plate. They still mean summer to me. I just can't have them as often as I used to.

INGREDIENTS

8 eggs, hard boiled

3 tablespoons mayonnaise, freshly made or Hellmann's

1 tablespoon Dijon mustard

¼ teaspoon chili powder

¼ teaspoon paprika, plus extra for garnish

Salt and freshly ground black pepper to taste

Gently peel the eggs, making sure that they remain whole. Slice each egg in half lengthwise. Carefully scoop out the yolks and place them in a small bowl. Arrange the whites, hollow-side up, on a flat plate or a deviled-egg plate.

Add the mayonnaise, mustard, chili powder, ¼ teaspoon paprika, salt, and pepper to the yolks, and mash together with a fork until smooth. Then, gently spoon an equal amount of the yolk mixture into each white. Or, you can be fancy and use a pastry bag to pipe the yolk mixture into the whites.

Lightly cover the plate with plastic wrap and refrigerate for 1 hour. Uncover, sprinkle each egg half with a little paprika, and serve chilled.

Tomato
Sandwiches

MAKES 2 SANDWICHES

Summer-ripened tomatoes are one of the joys of

the season. I buy them at the farmers' market, pick my own off the vines that I plant in early summer, and revel in those that I receive as gifts from friends or pick up at COMSOG, the local gardening co-op. This is one of the ways I serve them. It's a BLT without the B or the L. The trick is to use regular white bread: the squish of the bread is one of the pleasures of the sandwich.

Mix the mayonnaise with the basil in a small bowl. Place the bread slices on a work surface and spread each slice with an equal amount of the basil mayonnaise. Top 2 bread slices with the tomato slices, dividing them evenly. Place the other 2 bread slices, mayonnaise-side down, on top. Squish together, cut into quarters, and savor.

INGREDIENTS

1 tablespoon mayonnaise, freshly made or Hellmann's

½ teaspoon snipped fresh basil leaves

4 thin slices white bread

1 ripe tomato, thinly sliced

Stuffed Quahogs

1 cup water

1 cup Chardonnay or other dry white wine

24 quahogs (see Sources, page 198), scrubbed

1 cup *panko* (Japanese bread crumbs)

¼ cup crumbled saltine crackers (optional)

1 egg, beaten

1 tablespoon butter

1 small yellow onion, minced

2 scallions, including 2 inches of green tops, minced

3 tablespoons minced fresh flat-leaf parsley

½ teaspoon salt

½ teaspoon Bell's seasoning

½ teaspoon Old Bay seasoning

¼ teaspoon freshly ground black pepper

⅛ teaspoon cayenne pepper

Stuffed quahogs (the Vineyard's name for hard-shell

clams) were my father's favorite appetizer. On special occasions, he would get dressed in his favorite summer madras slacks and take us out to the Harborside Inn in Edgartown for sundown drinks, where we would sit on the deck. I would feed the ducks and sip my soft drink. He would have a martini and sit back and savor the restaurant's wonderful way with stuffed quahogs. This isn't the Harborside's recipe, but it comes close in taste, and I can never serve it without thinking of my father and the delight he took in watching the sun set over Edgartown Harbor as he ate stuffed quahogs. If you don't want to mail-order quahogs, you may use any hard-shell clams. They won't taste exactly like the Vineyard, but they will still be pretty darned good.

Preheat the oven to 350°F. Bring the water and wine to a boil in a 5-quart saucepan. Add the clams, discarding any that fail to close to the touch. Cover, return to a boil, and cook for 5 minutes. Uncover, remove any open clams with a slotted spoon, and then re-cover and continue to cook for 3 to 4 minutes longer, or until the remaining clams open. Remove them with the slotted spoon, discarding any that failed to open. When the clams are cool enough to handle, remove the meats from the shells and reserve the bottom shells. Mince the clam meats. Rinse and dry the reserved shells.

Combine the minced clams, *panko*, saltines (if using), and egg in a bowl and mix well. Melt the butter in a skillet over medium heat. Add the yellow onion and sauté for 5 minutes, or until lightly browned. Remove from the heat and add the sautéed onion to the clam mixture along with the scallions, parsley, salt, Bell's seasoning, Old Bay seasoning, black pepper, and cayenne pepper. Mix well.

Spoon the clam mixture into the reserved clam shells, dividing it evenly, and place the stuffed clams on a baking sheet. Bake for about 30 minutes, or until the tops are lightly browned. Serve hot.

Soups and **Salads**

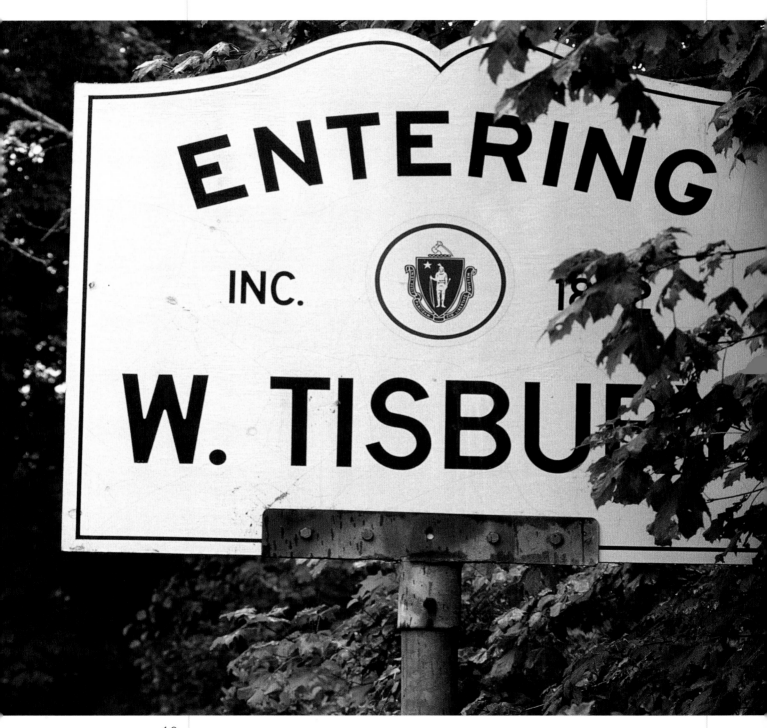

West Tisbury

A drive out of Tisbury through the nearby up-island

town of West Tisbury is like journeying into the New England of postcards. The white clapboard Congregational church shoots its spire skyward, while nearby townsfolk gossip on the porch of a general store that has been doing business since 1858. Venerable oaks shade the roadways and time seems to stand still. If it is summertime and a Saturday morning or Wednesday afternoon, the area around the Grange Hall is bustling with a popular farmers' market, and the riot of color and activity transforms New England into Provence.

Across from the church, statues of Junoesque dancers frolicking at the Field Gallery are a reminder of the island's artistic traditions. Antique shops vie for customers who want to bring their own little piece of Vineyard history home. Farming remains a major occupation on this part of the island, and West Tisbury's annual August Agriculture Fair reminds us of the island's past and shows off some of the best produce of the present farmers. The tiny town also seems to have a baking tradition, and anyone with a sweet tooth is sure to keep an eye out for the pie gazebo manned by relatives of Eileen Blake, the island's legendary pie maker.

Jamaican Red Pea Soup
with Spinners

1 pound (2 rounded cups) dried kidney beans

2 quarts water

½ cup finely chopped scallions, including 2 inches of green tops

2 sprigs fresh flat-leaf parsley, minced

2 sprigs fresh thyme, leaves stripped and minced

¼ cup minced celery

2 tablespoons minced garlic

2 cups minced cooked chicken

2 chicken bouillon cubes

Salt and freshly ground black pepper to taste

Spinners (recipe follows), optional

3 tablespoons minced Vidalia or other sweet onion

SPINNERS

½ cup flour

1 teaspoon salt

5 tablespoons water

It is quite a culinary jump from Jamaica to Martha's

Vineyard, but this soup and other dishes from the Caribbean increasingly turn up here. They appear on summer tables when travelers have returned from a visit to Jamaica, or when "African American" takes on its larger definition and someone in the family has Jamaican origins. But they show up year-round on the tables of Jamaicans who make the island their full-time home. Many of them arrived as migrant workers, then stayed on and took other jobs around the island. This soup is a wonderful one-pot meal for a cool night's dinner after a long day at the beach and can even be left simmering in the pot during the post-beach nap. The spinners are dumplings, while "red pea" is a Jamaican term for the kidney bean.

Pick over the beans and then soak them in cold water to cover overnight. The next day, drain the beans, place in a stockpot, and add the 2 quarts water, scallions, parsley, thyme, celery, garlic, chicken, and bouillon cubes. Season lightly with salt and pepper, cover, and bring to a boil over high heat. Lower the heat to a simmer and cook for 1 hour, or until the beans are tender.

Taste the soup and adjust the seasoning with salt and pepper. Add the spinners and continue to simmer for 5 minutes, or until the dumplings are cooked through. Ladle into bowls, garnish with the Vidalia onion, and serve.

To make the spinners, combine all of the ingredients together in a bowl and stir until you have a stiff, smooth dough. On a floured work surface, roll out the dough ¼ inch thick and cut into 12 equal pieces. Roll the pieces into cylinders, drop them into the simmering soup, and cook as directed.

Quahog Stew

6 tablespoons butter

1 onion, minced

2 cups milk

2 cups heavy cream

2 quarts shucked quahogs with their liquid (see Sources, page 198)

Pinch of ground mace

Salt and freshly ground black pepper to taste

The quahog, or hard-shell clam, was a part of the

diet of the Wampanoag, who made the island their home. It turns up in all manner of dishes, from clambakes to stews to roasts. This rich stew is great on a night when the autumn winds blow chilly and you want something warming. Serve the stew with oyster crackers or crusty bread.

Melt the butter in a heavy 5-quart saucepan over medium heat. Add the onion and sauté for about 3 minutes, or until translucent. Add the milk and cream and cook for 3 minutes. Add the quahogs and their liquid and the mace to the pan, reduce the heat to low, and simmer for about 3 minutes, or until the clams are plump.

Remove from the heat and season with salt and pepper. Ladle into bowls and serve piping hot.

Portuguese Kale Soup

This dish is a Vineyard standby. There are as many

recipes for it as there are Portuguese grandmothers on the island, and each version has its merits. This one is from Alice Coutinho. She has known me most of my life and was a great buddy of my mother's. We see each other at least once every summer to trade talk of the past and to share memories and recipes. This soup, like many soups, tastes better the next day, after the flavors have had time to meld. While linguiça is fairly easy to find, Portuguese *chouriço* is not as widely available. If you don't want to mail order it, you may substitute a mild Spanish chorizo. Serve the soup with crusty bread.

Rinse the kale well, then pick over and discard any tough stems and discolored spots. Cut the leaves crosswise into narrow strips and set aside.

Sauté the linguiça and *chouriço* in a stockpot over medium heat for 2 to 3 minutes, or until they have rendered some of their fat. Add the olive oil and onion and sauté for 3 minutes, or until the onion is translucent. Add the broth, cumin, salt, garlic, kale, cabbage, and water, raise the heat to medium-high, and bring to a boil. Lower the heat to a gentle simmer and cook for 1 hour, or until the kale and cabbage are very tender and the flavors have deepened and blended.

Add the potatoes and the kidney beans and their liquid and continue to cook for 15 minutes, or until the potatoes are fork-tender. Remove from the heat, let cool, cover, and refrigerate overnight.

The next day, skim off the fat from the surface and reheat the soup. Ladle into bowls and serve.

INGREDIENTS

1 pound kale

1 pound linguiça (see Sources, page 198), cut into ½-inch-thick slices

½ pound *chouriço* (see Sources, page 198), cut into ½-inch-thick slices

1 tablespoon olive oil

1 cup chopped onion

1 can (14 ounces) beef broth

½ teaspoon ground cumin

1½ teaspoons salt

1 clove garlic, minced

1 cup chopped green cabbage

2 quarts water

1 large or 2 medium Yukon Gold potatoes, peeled and diced (about 1 cup)

1 can (16 ounces) kidney beans with liquid

{ THE PORTUGUESE FESTA }

It begins with a whisper that circulates among the cognoscenti that the festa is this weekend. Down on Inkwell Beach, folks are savoring the last of the Saturday sun. On Circuit Avenue, diners are making their final restaurant decisions. Up on Vineyard Avenue at the Portuguese-American Club, preparations are finishing up for the annual event that celebrates the Portuguese heritage of the island: the Feast of the Holy Ghost, known to most simply as the Portuguese Festa.

The two-day celebration honors the fourteenth-century Queen Isabel of Portugal, who was known for her charitable ways. Her gesture is remembered with a feast and with the cooking of a traditional Portuguese kale soup, or *sopa*, that is sold on Saturday along with other Portuguese goodies, such as *malasadas*, or Portuguese crullers; and sandwiches of linguiça and *cacoila*, or Portuguese barbecue, pulled pork lightly seasoned with a salt-and-spice mix and serve on a roll with Kraft barbecue sauce or honey barbecue sauce on the side. For the unadventurous, there are hamburgers, cheeseburgers, and hot dogs, but the thing to have is a big bowl of *sopa*. It's a soup thick with linguiça slices, shredded kale, cabbage, and potatoes and garnished with sprigs of fresh mint. There are as many recipes for *sopa* as there are Portuguese families on the island, and each year the savvy tasters comment and judge.

By Sunday, the whole island knows. The festivities begin with a procession from the Steamship Authority Wharf, where Portuguese dancers from a sister community in New Bedford arrive. The parade forms and makes its way through town to the sounds of sirens, a marching band, and on some years the wail of a Portuguese bagpipe. There is an obligatory stop at Our Lady Star of the Sea Church for the blessing of the silver crown, the club's symbol in remembrance of Queen Isabel. It is carried by a lucky young girl who has received her first communion that year. Then, it's through town with a stop at the cemetery for the laying of a wreath, and up to the Portuguese-American Hall, where the party starts all over again.

If Saturday night is for the adults, Sunday afternoon is for family groups who come together to sample the dishes and pass on the feeling of community and conviviality across generations. Whether Saturday's evening event or Sunday's family outing, the Portuguese Festa is the highpoint of July for many, but Vineyarders and seasonal visitors alike know that the *sopa* is always better on the second day, and on Sunday it is free.

Simple Summer Green Salad
with Lemon Vinaigrette

1 tablespoon freshly
squeezed lemon juice

3 tablespoons extra-virgin
olive oil

¼ teaspoon freshly grated
lemon zest

Pinch of sugar

Salt and freshly ground black
pepper to taste

SALAD

5 to 6 ounces mixed baby
salad greens

3 scallions, including 3 inches
of green tops, minced

I'm not sure why, but summer in Martha's Vineyard

brings out the salad eater in me. I scarf down tomatoes as though I'll never see another sun-warmed one, I crave the coleslaw I detested as a child, and I'll even dip a fork into a bowl of potato salad more than once. At heart, though, I'm a purist, and nothing beats the classic mixed green salad, especially if the greens are as pristine and as fresh as they are when they come from North Tabor Farm or Whippoorwill Farm, two purveyors of the Vineyard's finest. Then, it just doesn't get any better.

To make the vinaigrette, combine all of the ingredients in a small bowl and whisk to mix well.

To make the salad, rinse the greens, dry well, and place in a salad bowl. Add the scallions, drizzle on the vinaigrette, toss, and serve.

Arugula and Love Apple
Salad

2 bunches arugula

2 tomatoes, quartered

1 small sweet onion such as Vidalia or Maui, thinly sliced

Vinaigrette of your choice

Salt and freshly ground black pepper to taste

All summer long, I indulge in my love of fresh

greens with salad lunches. One day, I'll have a Niçoise prepared with leftover fish from the previous night's dinner; another, I'll stick to just greens; and on some, I'll indulge in this simple blend of arugula and love apples (or tomatoes, as they're better known to us all). The bite of the tangy greens is the perfect foil for the slight sweetness of the summer-ripe tomatoes.

Scrupulously rinse the arugula leaves, as they tend to be sandy, and discard any yellowed leaves or woody stems. Place the arugula in a salad bowl. Add the tomatoes and onion, drizzle with the vinaigrette, and toss to mix. Season to taste with salt and pepper and serve immediately.

Mushroom and Parmesan Salad

This is a variation of a dish that was offered to me

as an *amuse-gueule* at Lilette Restaurant in New Orleans. There, it was prepared with porcini mushrooms that had been shaved paper-thin on a mandoline. Because porcini not only cost forty dollars a pound, but also aren't available fresh on Martha's Vineyard, I came up with this poor man's version, which I gladly gobble down on my own and serve to guests.

Mound the thinly sliced mushrooms on a platter. Top them with the Parmesan and then scatter the lemon zest on top.

To make a vinaigrette, combine the lemon juice and olive oil in a small bowl and whisk to mix well. Drizzle the vinaigrette over the mushrooms and cheese. Season with salt and pepper and serve immediately.

INGREDIENTS

½ pound baby bella (cremini) mushrooms, thinly sliced

¼ cup freshly shaved Parmesan cheese

⅛ teaspoon freshly grated lemon zest

1 teaspoon freshly squeezed lemon juice

1½ tablespoons extra-virgin olive oil

Salt and freshly ground black pepper to taste

Rice Salad

I cooked up this rice salad for a party for the artist

John Scott in New Orleans, then experimented with the theme in Martha's Vineyard later that year, embellishing it for other friends at summer gatherings. This is the version that we all liked the best. If you don't like asparagus, you may substitute 1 cup cooked peas.

Place the rice in a serving bowl. Add the parsley and asparagus and stir to mix well.

To make the dressing, combine the anchovies and their oil, garlic, olive oil, and vinegar in a small bowl and whisk to mix well. Season with salt and pepper. Pour the dressing over the rice mixture, toss lightly with a fork to distribute the dressing evenly, cover with plastic wrap, and let sit for 1 hour. Serve at room temperature.

INGREDIENTS

3 cups cooked white rice, at room temperature

¼ cup chopped fresh parsley

½ pound asparagus, trimmed, cooked until tender-crisp, and cut into 1½-inch pieces

1 can (2 ounces) flat anchovy fillets in olive oil, drained, with oil reserved, and minced

½ teaspoon minced garlic

2 tablespoons olive oil

1 tablespoon balsamic vinegar

Salt and freshly ground black pepper to taste

{ FARMERS' MARKET }

I have loudly proclaimed my love of farmers' markets and will miss no opportunity to visit one, whichever continent I'm on. They're the perfect locus for people-watching, and what cook would miss the chance to pinch and prod the wares or talk with the growers who display their goods with such pride of ownership? My personal seasons are defined by the markets in New York, Martha's Vineyard, and New Orleans, and by my travels throughout the year. Martha's Vineyard is the home of my summer market. I'm a real New Yorker and a nondriver, so my friends all know that on Wednesdays and Saturdays from July to September, I'm going to be a nuisance and beg a ride to the grounds surrounding the old Agricultural Hall (now the Grange Hall) in West Tisbury, the site of the local farmers' market.

There, in a tumble of color, the island's farmers strut their stuff. The market season begins slowly, with a handful of trucks and vans backed up to the shopping area, their owners bringing in tomato plants and herbs ready for setting out and a few of the early harvested vegetables. By July things are ramping up, with zinnias appearing to signal the colors of summer and the early crop of island corn that becomes the leitmotif of my summer

cooking. August brings full swing and the market is bursting with bunches of huge sunflowers and fragrant oriental lilies. The greens are in and the baby bok choy and Asian mix from Bluebird Way are ready, if I get there early enough. I trawl for greens from Whippoorwill Farm and delight in finding new items like purple scallions or the surprise of Cape gooseberries and tomatillos. I always keep a container or two of Pam's Pesto in the fridge in case of last-minute company or an attack of pre-dinner laziness. And, of course, there's the lemon-limeade that quenches thirst and means the farmers' market to me. (I can't quite do the wheatgrass juice.)

By September, the island's bounty is bursting. On the weekend trips that I make to the Vineyard until Columbus Day, I'm a Saturday problem for friends, as I stock up on items that will keep the island's tastes alive for me during the winter. I lug home pounds of slightly bruised tomatoes for chutney and purchase a few of the specially made mustards that I give as gifts or that add zing to my own winter meals. When the pumpkins appear, I know it's time to think of the year's final trips to the island and of saying good-bye to the market, scratching the last Lab nose, and calculating how long I can make the greens last.

Then I catch the ferry in the rented minivan crammed full of books, cats, coolers packed with produce, jars of chutneys, and a pumpkin or two squeezed in for good measure, and ride back to New York to savor my bounty and to think about what I'll find in the market next year.

Good Old Iceberg *with* Blue Cheese Dressing

SERVES 6

Iceberg lettuce is the Rodney Dangerfield of the

lettuce family: it just doesn't get any respect. I don't eat it often, but I always keep a head of it in my refrigerator. It holds up better than the more delicate greens, which means that it will be there waiting for me when I return from a trip ravenous for something crisp and green. Then I whip up a batch of blue cheese dressing, slather it on a chunk of iceberg, and remind myself what a salad used to be in the days before mesclun and arugula were available everywhere.

Cut out the core from the lettuce and cut the head into 6 wedges. Place the wedges on a serving platter and sprinkle the tomato and onion over them.

To make the dressing, combine the blue cheese, yogurt, and 1 tablespoon milk in a small bowl and cream together with a fork until a smooth paste forms. You may have to add a bit more milk to get the consistency you want.

Slather the blue cheese dressing over the iceberg wedges and serve immediately.

INGREDIENTS

1 head iceberg lettuce

1 tomato, peeled, seeded, and coarsely chopped

1 small Vidalia or other sweet onion, sliced

3 tablespoons crumbled Roquefort, Saga, or other blue-veined cheese

3 tablespoons plain yogurt

1 tablespoon milk, or as needed

Cucumber Salad

INGREDIENTS

3 large cucumbers, peeled and very thinly sliced

2 sweet onions such as Vidalia or Maui, thinly sliced

4 small allspice berries, cracked

½ cup cider vinegar

2 tablespoons brown sugar, or to taste

1 tablespoon water

My mother made this salad every summer. Just

seeing a really fresh cucumber and smelling its almost-violet perfume makes me think of this cooling, slightly sweet slurry of slippery cuke and onion.

Alternately layer the sliced cucumbers and onions in a glass bowl.

To make the dressing, combine the allspice berries, vinegar, 2 tablespoons brown sugar, and water in a small bowl and whisk to mix well. Taste and adjust with more sugar if you like. Pour the sweetened vinegar over the cucumbers.

Cover the salad with a plate that fits just inside the bowl, place a 1-pound weight on the plate, and refrigerate the salad for 3 hours.

When ready to serve, remove the weight and plate, fluff the salad with a fork, and serve chilled.

Martha Mae's
Caesar Salad

Martha Mae Jones is a friend with a summer

birthday, and each year I used to agonize about her gift. Then one day she told me that the only present she ever wanted from me was the promise that I would make her an annual birthday Caesar salad. I made the promise, and every summer in August, Martha gets her Caesar. My version is made without croutons and includes a raw egg, which authorities regularly caution should not be eaten by very young children, pregnant women, older people, or anyone with a compromised immune system. Martha and I are of a certain age and healthy enough to believe that we can stand a raw egg from time to time with no ill effects. Don't try this salad unless you can too.

Cut away the core of each romaine head and rinse the heads well, discarding any blemished leaves. Tear the leaves into 2-inch pieces and place in a salad bowl.

To make the dressing, combine the egg and anchovy fillets and their oil and muddle together with a fork until you have a viscous mixture and the anchovy fillets are almost completely dissolved. Gradually add the olive oil and lemon juice, whisking constantly. Season with pepper.

Pour the dressing over the romaine leaves. Top with the Parmesan cheese and toss to mix. Serve immediately.

INGREDIENTS

2 heads romaine lettuce

1 egg

1 can (2 ounces) flat anchovy fillets in olive oil, undrained

4 tablespoons extra-virgin olive oil

2 tablespoons freshly squeezed lemon juice

Freshly ground black pepper to taste

2 tablespoons freshly grated Parmesan cheese

{ NOT BY BREAD ALONE }

"Man does not live by bread alone," so the old dictum goes, but you couldn't prove it on the Vineyard, where people flock to their favorite bakeries with the assiduity of scallop shell–bedecked pilgrims heading to Santiago de Compostela. There seem to be an inordinate number of bakers and bakeries on the island, each with its own specialty that is well worth the up-island or down-island drive. Humphrey's, Osprey, Scottish Bakehouse, and the legendary Black Dog each have their stalwart partisans, and issues such as rent renewals, shopping policies, and changes in ownership are headline news in the local papers.

In my youth, the bakery in Oak Bluffs was named Wamsley's, and I delighted in the hermits, apple squares, freshly made doughnuts, soft flaky dinner rolls, and round cookies filled with chips of toffee that were sold there. In the same spot—right next to the post office—five decades or so later, baked goods are still sold, but Martha's Vineyard Gourmet Café & Bakery adds croissants and muffins and mocha cakes and tarts.

The constant remains doughnuts, especially the Oak Bluffs tradition of backdoor doughnuts. Every evening after nine, while the bakers are at work whisking up the next day's confections, you can head through the parking lot to get backdoor doughnuts. Still warm from the fryer, they can trump the fancier desserts of most island restaurants and are the perfect way to end an evening.

Up-island or down-, the baker who is universally recognized as the Vineyard's foremost pie maker is Eileen Blake, who has been baking and selling her sublime pies since the early 1970s. They used to be available only at the gingerbread-bedecked gazebo just outside of her house on State Road, but now they can be bought at several supermarkets on the island. That means that we can all feast on her burgundy pie, made with a mix of blueberries and cranberries; her oh-so-Southern chess pie; or her old-fashioned strawberry-rhubarb pie. They're all flaky crusted and taste of grandma's kitchen. In fact, they are so homemade good that many cooks have been tempted to pass off one of Eileen Blake's pies as their own on this island, where the prayer for daily bread must be expanded to include cookies, doughnuts, and pies.

{ THE COUNTY AGRICULTURAL FAIR }

I have a small shadow box that I keep in my office. In it are a series of ceramic buttons that were one of my mother's creative passions, along with the blue ribbon that she won for them at the Martha's Vineyard Agricultural Fair. Held in West Tisbury, the Ag Fair, as it is popularly called, is a Vineyard fixture, a place where local artists and crafters can gain praise for their work. It is where the Vineyard returns to its rural past, turning back the clock to calmer, quieter times. The fair offers not only prizes for quilts, crafts, and wildflower arranging, but also gives awards for spectacular vegetables and items like preserves, chutneys, pies, and jams.

A testimonial to the Vineyard's agricultural roots, the fair also holds oxen pulls and sheepshearing contests, connecting the island's bedrock agricultural residents with the city-slicker summer folks who have adopted its bucolic ways. This is a place where the 4-H crowd meets up with the Wall Street set, with each bringing a special sense of wonder at the magnificent bounty of their favorite island.

Entering an item for judging is taken seriously and is not for the fainthearted. Families compete over decades, taking great pride in knowing that their zucchini are the best on the island and their beach plum preserves have earned a blue ribbon. Some continue the tradition of entering as a testimonial to the gardening know-how of a family member who has gone on to glory.

On opening day, there is hushed anticipation as the cedar-shingled Agricultural Hall is cordoned off while the judging takes place. And the competition is fierce. Outside, folks keep busy scarfing down non-Vineyard food like kettle corn, funnel cakes, and corn dogs and watching the dressage competitions in the outdoor rings. Inside, the judges are tasting and selecting the year's winners, a task that involves equal measures of finely tuned taste buds and a cast-iron stomach. Then the doors are opened and the rush is on to see who garnered the top prizes.

My favorite part of the fair is the decidedly non-PC skillet-throwing contest, which draws women from all over the island to see who can toss a heavy skillet the farthest. I'm far too sensitive ever to consider entering my summer tomato chutney, but one day I may have a hand at tossing a skillet. I think I might manage to get that one right.

Condiments

Chilmark

Sheep farms and rolling hills that recall the Scottish moors surround Chilmark, perhaps the most bucolic of the island's towns. Moss-covered stone fences separate properties and venerable oaks provide sun-dappled views. Like West Tisbury, its sister up-island town, Chilmark boasts a white clapboard church with a tall spire, but the community's quiet country air makes its island neighbor to the north seem almost urban. A small set of shops forms the town center, and Cornerway, Bittersweet, and Theo's restaurants lure evening travelers out onto the town's winding roads.

Most folks who head to Chilmark in search of matters culinary are on their way to Chilmark Chocolates, housed in a yellow gingerbread house at the side of the road. Chocolate-covered blueberries (in season) and bittersweet chocolate–dipped candied ginger make the cars stop and the lines form. Open year-round with a break in January, the shop has helped many full-time residents safely through the dark winter nights and has made Chilmark a must-stop place on the island's culinary map.

Cranberry Chutney

INGREDIENTS

1½ cups fresh or frozen cranberries

1-inch piece fresh ginger, peeled and coarsely chopped

2 cloves garlic, minced

2 teaspoons freshly minced orange zest

1 teaspoon minced jalapeño chile, or to taste

½ cup freshly squeezed lemon juice

½ cup sugar

Cranberries are iconic in this part of the world,

and it's only natural that they turn up on my table as a chutney that I eat not only at Thanksgiving, but all year long.

Place the cranberries, ginger, garlic, orange zest, and chile in a food processor and pulse until you have a grainy paste. (You may have to add a bit of the lemon juice to get it started.) Spoon the mixture into a 1-quart nonreactive saucepan. Add the lemon juice and sugar and stir to make sure that all of the ingredients are evenly mixed.

Place over medium heat and bring to a boil. Lower the heat and simmer uncovered, stirring occasionally, for 25 to 30 minutes, or until the mixture has a jamlike consistency. Be sure to stir all the way to the bottom of the pan, or the chutney may stick and scorch.

Remove from the heat and allow to cool to room temperature. Spoon into a serving dish and serve.

Tomato
Chutney

There's nothing that can match the taste of summer-

ripe tomatoes. The farmers' market in West Tisbury has them in cartons around mid-July, and they just get better as the season goes on, until about the time I take the boat back to "America." Before I go, I sometimes make a detour to Norton's farm stand and get a few more for New York eating. I have usually already made some batches of my tomato chutney to keep me going until my return. I serve it with everything from hot dogs (page 111) to grilled chicken to steak, and I usually dole it out so that I'm finishing up my last precious jar just about the time that I head back to the Vineyard for another summer.

Place the tomatoes, ginger, chiles, onions, and garlic in a food processor and pulse until the mixture is the consistency of a thick liquid. Pour into a heavy nonreactive saucepan, add the raisins, brown sugar, and vinegar, and stir to mix well. Place over medium heat and bring to a boil. Lower the heat to a simmer and cook uncovered, stirring occasionally, for about 1½ hours, or until the mixture has a jamlike consistency.

Remove from the heat, let cool to room temperature, transfer to a serving bowl, and serve. Leftovers can be kept in a tightly covered jar in the refrigerator for up to 2 weeks.

NOTE: If you have a bumper crop of tomatoes, you can make a larger batch of the chutney, ladle it hot into scalded half-pint or pint jars, seal with canning lids, and process in a hot-water bath for 10 minutes. Check the seals and if they are good, store the chutney in a cool, dark place for up to 1 year. Otherwise, store in the refrigerator for up to 2 weeks.

INGREDIENTS

12 large, ripe tomatoes, peeled and sliced

2-inch piece fresh ginger, peeled and coarsely chopped

2 jalapeño chiles, or to taste

2 1arge onions, quartered

2 cloves garlic, minced

½ cup dark raisins

1 cup firmly packed brown sugar

1 cup distilled white vinegar

Watermelon Rind Pickles

9 cups cubed watermelon rind (1-inch cubes)

½ cup salt

2 quarts plus 2 cups water

1¾ cups cider vinegar

½ cup balsamic vinegar

2 cups firmly packed dark brown sugar

1 lemon, thinly sliced

2 cinnamon sticks, crushed

1 teaspoon whole cloves

2 teaspoons allspice berries, cracked

Over four decades ago, I saw my first-ever restaurant

salad bar in Munro's Boston House on Circuit Avenue in Oak Bluffs. Then the summit of Vineyard dining, Munro's was the kind of island place where jackets were required and an elegant hostess ushered diners to their tables.

One summer my Uncle Jim wowed the crowd and challenged the dress code by wearing charcoal gray Bermuda shorts in formal Bermuda style, complete with blazer and knee socks. But even he didn't make as big an impression as the salad bar. It was situated in the Charcoal Galley, where steaks and chops were the thing, and contained not only salad fixings like lettuce, tomato, and onions, but also condiments, including corn relish and watermelon rind pickles.

Munro's has long since morphed into the Atlantic Connection nightclub, but the memory lingers on, and I content myself with making my own watermelon rind pickles each summer. You'll need to start with a watermelon that weighs about 3 pounds to yield this amount of rind.

As you prepare the watermelon rind for cubing, be sure to remove all the green skin and all but a small amount of the red meat. Combine the salt and 2 quarts of the water in a bowl large enough to accommodate the cubed rind and stir to dissolve the salt. Submerge the rind in the brine and let soak overnight.

Drain the rind, rinse with fresh water, and drain again. Place the rind in a large nonreactive saucepan, add water to cover, and place over medium heat. Bring to a simmer and cook, uncovered, for 15 minutes, or until fork-tender.

Meanwhile, combine the remaining 2 cups water, cider vinegar, balsamic vinegar, brown sugar, lemon slices, cinnamon, cloves, and allspice in another large nonreactive saucepan and bring to a boil over medium-high heat, stirring occasionally to dissolve the sugar. Lower the heat to a simmer and cook for 15 minutes, or until a thin syrup forms.

Drain the watermelon rind, add it to the simmering syrup, and continue to simmer for about 20 minutes, or until the rind is translucent. Using a slotted spoon, transfer the rind to hot sterilized canning jars. Ladle in the hot unstrained syrup to cover, allowing about $^1/_4$-inch headroom, then cover tightly.

Process the jars in a hot-water bath for 15 minutes. Remove from the water bath, let cool, and check the seal. If you find a jar without a good seal, store it in the refrigerator; it will keep for up to 1 month. Store jars with a good seal in a cool, dark place for up to several months—if they last that long.

{ THE PORTUGUESE PRESENCE }

"Fala português?" Well, you can on the Vineyard. Portuguese from the Azores have been on the island for centuries and were celebrated among the whalers. They were followed by the Cape Verdeans, who left their mark as well. But no native Portuguese speakers have changed the day-to-day finds in the supermarkets as much as the recently arrived Brazilians.

First appearing on the island in the 1990s, perhaps lured by the presence of a Portuguese-speaking community, the Brazilians, mainly from the states of Minas Gerais and Espíritu Santo, have become the island's new service professionals, taking their place alongside the Jamaicans, who arrived as migrant workers; the Irish, who journeyed to serve as hotel employees; and the eastern Europeans, who come each summer to drive the island's buses and do seasonal work in shops. But while a Ting, the Jamaican grapefruit soda, can occasionally be found at the Stop & Shop, and a piece of Irish soda bread may turn up around St. Patrick's Day, no group has had a major influence on the availability of foods and restaurants on the island like the Brazilians.

At my grocery store in Oak Bluffs, I am thrilled that I can now find guava juice and cashew juice, and kilo bags of the salt rubs used for *churrasco*, alongside Boston baked beans. I can find malagueta chiles and dendê oil, and even yucca in the section that stocks potatoes and onions. There are linguiça and *chouriço* and jars of coconut sweets, or *cocadas*, flavored with prune or passionfruit. I spend my summers indulging in dried mango and cans of coconut water. (All of this in a shop where fresh arugula only arrived a few years back!)

In Brazilian specialty shops, there are all sorts of cookies and crackers that I haven't seen since my days in Bahia and Rio, as well as frozen Brazilian *pão de queijo*, a delicious cheese bread served as an appetizer in most Brazilian restaurants. Brazilians are also among the few groups who have influenced the local restaurant scene, whether through their own places or special Brazilian nights at other restaurants.

The stepladder of immigrant success in this country will see the Brazilians move up and off to other occupations on the island and beyond. But one thing is sure: they have changed the island's food in many ways and we are all much better for it.

Brazilian Hot Sauce

½ cup freshly squeezed lime juice

½ cup freshly squeezed lemon juice

2 teaspoons minced fresh flat-leaf parsley

2 teaspoons minced onion

1 teaspoon minced fresh cilantro

Minced preserved malagueta chile (see Sources, page 198) or other hot chile to taste

Salt and freshly ground black pepper to taste

I discovered this lemon-and-lime-based sauce on

one of my early trips to Brazil, where it is eaten with grilled meats and roasts. I like it drizzled over steamed vegetables or served with greens, whether they're served in the African American or Brazilian style. The sauce is easy to prepare and will keep for a few days in the refrigerator.

Combine all of the ingredients in a small non-reactive bowl and stir to mix well. Cover with plastic wrap and let stand for 30 minutes to allow the flavors to blend. Serve at room temperature.

Vinegared Chiles

This is a simple table condiment of the sort that

I always have on hand all summer long. The chiles are great added to any soup or stew for flavor, and the vinegar itself can be a hot sauce that is perfect over Brazilian greens or just about anything else that can use a savory hit.

Place the chiles in a quart jar (or smaller jars) with a tight-fitting lid. Mix together the cider and balsamic vinegars and pour over the chiles to cover. Seal the jar(s) tightly and place on a sunny windowsill for 3 days. The chiles will flavor the vinegar.

Open the jar(s) and serve as a condiment or a hot sauce. Once opened, store in the refrigerator.

INGREDIENTS

1 pound jalapeño chiles, well rinsed and cut into 1-inch-thick rounds

2 cups cider vinegar

1 cup balsamic vinegar

Classic Vinaigrette
with a Twist

2 tablespoons olive oil

1 tablespoon red wine vinegar

½ teaspoon minced garlic

1 teaspoon minced anchovy fillets

½ teaspoon oil from the anchovy fillets

½ teaspoon Dijon mustard

Among the things that I love best about my

Martha's Vineyard summers are the fresh salad greens on the island. I can never decide whether I prefer the greens from Whippoorwill Farm or North Tabor Farm. Then there are the greens that are sold from a cooler in front of the Bittersweet restaurant in West Tisbury. Currently my favorite greens are an Asian mix from Bluebird Way. I only know that a day on the Vineyard without a fresh green salad is not a good day for me.

I always make my own dressing for the greens and love experimenting with different ingredients. This vinaigrette has been a winner for several summers. The "twist" is the addition of minced anchovies and a bit of the anchovy oil. You may not have the island's greens, but you'll be fine if you use greens from your own garden or the freshest ones available in the market.

Combine all of the ingredients in a small jar or bottle, cover tightly, and shake well to mix.

Seafood Boil

You can use this all-purpose mix of seasonings

for everything from crabs to crayfish. I even sometimes pulverize it to a fine powder and use it to season fried fish. It will keep in a tightly stoppered container on a cupboard shelf for an entire summer.

Place all of the ingredients in a spice grinder and pulverize until you have a coarse powder. Stir to mix and to make sure no large unprocessed pieces remain. Pour the mixture into a glass jar, cap tightly, and store in a cool, dark place.

¼ cup pickling spice

2 tablespoons brown mustard seeds

2 tablespoons black peppercorns

3 tablespoons coarse sea salt

1 tablespoon celery seeds

1 tablespoon dried chives

2 teaspoons crushed red chiles, or to taste

1 teaspoon ground ginger

5 bay leaves, broken into pieces

2 teaspoons dried Italian oregano

{BEACHES}

I hope that I will always live where I can see the swoop of seagulls. Something about being near the water makes my heart sing. Strangely, though I have summered near beaches for over five decades, and have visited some of the world's best for over forty years, I've never really enjoyed them. It may have something to do with being unceremoniously ushered off Edgartown's beach in my youth. The good townspeople, it seemed, knew that the most patrician of Vineyard towns had no black residents and gently reminded my parents and me that the little curve of beach that we had selected for that day's outing was reserved for Edgartown residents only. We retreated to "our" beach up the street, just a few minutes' walk from our home. It was known—at first clandestinely and now proudly—as the Inkwell, for obvious reasons. Since that time, I've always been more than a bit ambivalent about the water's edge.

Sand has traditionally been a part of the problem, too. I find that it is one of the most irritatingly rude elements invented by Mother Nature. No matter how hard I try to dust it off and wash it out, it sinks into corners and crevices that I didn't know I had, to remain and irritate.

As a result, I've become a seaside philosopher of sorts, observing the behavior of beachgoers as though I were a Victorian naturalist watching the antics of some alien tribe. They are divided into three types: the sporty ones, the social ones, and those who seek only seclusion. They share the beach companionably, each group with its own hours and its own rituals.

I swim little. However, I secretly admire the people who do, flowing back and forth with the precision of aquacade dancers: arms rhythmically cleaving the ultramarine water as they glide between gently lapping waves. They are the sporty ones whose days are punctuated with exercises on the beach and sunrise swims.

The second types are rampant in Oak Bluffs. They are the social beachgoers. They occupy the beach, landing like the Allies on D-Day, complete with chairs and umbrellas, radios and coolers filled with a day's nourishment, ready to camp out amid friends playing bid whist, gossiping, and nibbling. The chatting is interrupted only when the heat of the sun's rays makes a brief dip obligatory. These folks are not here for the water. Rather, the water provides a locus for conversation and for coming together.

I number myself among the final type of beachgoers. We come out when the beach is closing down for the day. The chairs have been packed up and the buckets loaded back into the SUVs, along with the kids and umbrellas and leftover food. The beach is no longer as pristine as it is in early morning, but Iemanjá (the Yoruba goddess of salt water) does her work rapidly, and calm returns even amid the few bits of lingering detritus. The beach is peaceful in the early evening. Seagulls hover and dive looking for any morsels left behind, and dog walkers throw one last stick for their dripping Labradors. The only sound is the quiet lapping of the waves.

I'll find a rock that is not too sandy, leave my belongings, and wade in singing softly to the ocean. If all is well, the waves will rush up to meet me, welcoming me back for yet another year. I shiver at the first touch of the frigid water, then gradually acclimatize and walk back and forth at surf's edge, singing and dancing to the sea that is the mother of us all. I usually leave a gift—some coins or a flower. Then I turn, gather my belongings, and head back up the road. I've made my peace with the water for yet another year.

Main Dishes

{ MAIN DISHES }

Menemsha

A photographer's dream and a fish lover's

nirvana, Menemsha is actually a village within the township of Chilmark. However, it has a personality so large that it seems to be a town in itself to anyone who has ever been on the Dutcher Dock when the fishing boats come in and unload containers full of flopping fish still glistening with seawater. This is a place where the men who go down to the sea in ships rule.

For generations, many summer families have come to dine on the local catch at the elegant Beach Plum Inn or the more casual Home Port. Sundown is prime time for Menemsha dining, and some spots pack their guests' meals to go so they can sit on the beach to eat them. Another option is late-afternoon lunch at Larsen's Fish Market, a place that also cheerfully sells some of the island's best fish. At Larsen's, you can buy a pound or two of harpooned swordfish or a tub of house-made bluefish spread, or you can wait while your lobsters are steamed to order. Many summer friends make an afternoon of it and sit outside on the lobster pots, savoring the crustaceans straight from the pot along with freshly shucked clams.

Whatever the venue—on the dock, on the beach, in a restaurant, at home—Menemsha meals celebrate the sea that provided the island's livelihood for centuries.

Marvino's
One-Pot Lobster Feast

SERVES 4

For a few years, my friend Marvin Jones

operated the only black-owned restaurant on the Vineyard. It was called Lobster in the Bluffs and was a special spot on Circuit Avenue in Oak Bluffs. Marvin specialized in a one-pot shore dinner that he had perfected. Unfortunately, Lobster in the Bluffs is now only a corner of a smile in the hazy memories of summers past, but I persuaded him to give up his recipe. You won't get the fellowship or the fun, but you can create your own memories over this lobster.

Select a pot large enough to accommodate all the ingredients. Place the potatoes in the pot with water to cover by about 2 inches, cover, and place over medium heat. Bring to a simmer and cook for 10 minutes. Add the linguiça, corn, and lobsters and continue to steam for 4 minutes. Add the mussels and clams, discarding any that fail to close to the touch, and continue to steam for 4 to 6 minutes longer, or until the lobster tails and heads begin to separate and the clams and mussels open (see Note). Discard any mussels and clams that failed to open.

Serve immediately with melted butter for dipping the lobster meat, a cup of the cooking broth for dunking the steamers and mussels, and the lemons. Reserve the remaining cooking broth for other uses, such as Marvino's Lobster Grits (page 142).

NOTE: If the clams and mussels open before the lobsters are cooked, remove them and serve them as an appetizer, or place them on a serving platter and reserve until the lobster is done.

INGREDIENTS

12 small new potatoes

½ pound linguiça (see Sources, page 198), cut into 1-inch pieces

4 ears corn, shucked and cut in half

4 live lobsters, about 1½ pounds each

20 mussels, scrubbed, soaked in salted water to cover for 2 to 3 hours to expel sand, and beards removed

12 steamer clams, scrubbed and soaked in salted water for 2 to 3 hours to expel sand

Melted butter for serving

Lemon wedges for serving

Scallop Rolls

INGREDIENTS

4 tablespoons butter

2 pounds bay scallops
(see Sources, page 198)

¼ cup finely minced celery

1 teaspoon finely minced
onion

About ¼ cup mayonnaise,
freshly made or Hellmann's

6 New England frankfurter
rolls (see Sources, page 198)

Salt and freshly ground
black pepper to taste

Most folks know that New England is the home of

the lobster roll. But it is also the home of the scallop roll, delicately cooked scallops lightly bound with mayonnaise and then placed in a toasted New England frankfurter roll. The frankfurter roll is special because it is like a permanently folded piece of bread that allows for toasting on the outside, which means lots more taste. The same roll adds a New England flair to all of the Vineyard's franks. To my mind, this more unusual roll is as good as a lobster roll and can be made from either freshly sautéed or leftover scallops. I'm more likely to have leftover scallops than lobster meat, so it is easier to make, too.

Melt 1 tablespoon of the butter in a heavy skillet over medium-high heat. Add half of the scallops and cook, stirring occasionally, for 3 to 5 minutes, or until the scallops are lightly browned on all sides. Transfer the scallops to a bowl and repeat with another tablespoon of the butter and the remaining scallops.

Let the scallops cool and then add the celery and onion and mix well. Gradually add the mayonnaise, making sure that the scallop salad is neither too wet nor too dry; each family has its preference. When you have reached the desired consistency, stop. Cover with plastic wrap and refrigerate for 1 hour so the flavors will blend.

When you are ready to serve, melt the remaining 2 tablespoons butter in a large skillet over medium-high heat. Working in batches if necessary, add the frankfurter rolls and toast until nicely golden on both sides.

Season the scallop salad with salt and pepper, and then immediately fill the hot rolls and serve.

Fried Scup

12 medium-sized porgies

¼ cup freshly squeezed lemon juice

Canola oil for frying

½ cup mayonnaise, freshly made or Hellmann's

1 tablespoon Seafood Boil (page 77)

¼ cup yellow cornmeal

¼ cup flour

Salt and freshly ground black pepper to taste

When we first arrived on the Vineyard, my parents

and I were confused by the term *scup* on the chalkboards in fish markets. What was this strange new fish? It turns out that it is simply a regional term for the porgy, a favorite fish of African Americans. Here, the fish is given the traditional Southern treatment and fried to a golden brown. The recipe includes a twist that my mother learned from a Vineyard fisherman: a slathering of mayonnaise helps the cornmeal to adhere and adds to the taste. Scup, once common, is now a limited catch, so check the rules in your neighborhood, then enjoy.

Have the fishmonger clean the porgies and remove the heads and fins.

Place the fish in a large nonreactive bowl and sprinkle them with the lemon juice. Cover and let sit while you heat the oil and prepare the coating.

Pour the oil to a depth of about 2 inches into a deep cast-iron skillet and heat to 350°F on a deep-frying thermometer. While the oil is heating, pulverize the Seafood Boil to a fine powder in a spice grinder. Combine it with the cornmeal, flour, and salt and pepper in a brown paper bag.

Place the fish, a few at a time, in the bag and shake well to coat evenly. Working in batches, slide the fish into the hot oil, being careful not to crowd them in the pan. Fry, turning once, for 2 to 3 minutes on each side, or until golden brown. Transfer to paper towels to drain, then place on a warmed platter. Repeat until all the fish are cooked. Serve at once.

{ BASS AND BLUEFISH FOR FREE }

Quansoo, Wasque, Norton's Point, Stonewall—the names of the up-island and down-island beaches are the fishermen's litany of special spots. They can be seen casting into the surf, silently praying that the winds and tides are favorable. The three *b*'s—bass, bonito, and bluefish—are the goal of the island's hardcore fisherfolk. Every September, their special spots and others like them around the island are the Holy Grail to anyone entered in the annual Martha's Vineyard Striped Bass and Bluefish Derby.

For the month after the close of the summer season, the island turns to thoughts of fishing. The five-week tournament is more than a simple fishing competition. It is an island-wide event, with bait and tackle shops and charter boats placing advertisements in the two local papers. From on and off the island, thousands come to enter the derby and battle the wily piscatorial prey. (In 2005, there were more than twenty-eight hundred entrants.)

Late in the day when the boats are in, the weigh station at the Edgartown Harbor draws onlookers reflecting every aspect of Vineyard life, from shoulder-season strollers to derby fanatics hoping to see the weigh-in of a fifty-pound behemoth. Those in the running scan the posted results, hoping that they have not been bested in their category by a new arrival, and peer to see who will wear the small gold pins on their caps that signal first-place daily winners. Others quietly query in hope of finding out what the legendary island fishermen have brought in.

Still others, older islanders all, watch knowingly and run through their mental Rolodexes of bass and bluefish recipes. They know that during the weeks of the derby, the bass, bluefish, and bonito that don't head home with the anglers are distributed free at the island's senior citizens' centers. In that way, while the photos are being taken and congratulations go out to the winners, even the landlubbers and those who have never placed bait on a hook or cast into the roiling surf get to share in the bounty of the sea.

Grilled Swordfish Skewers

SERVES 4

INGREDIENTS

1 swordfish steak, about
1 pound and 1½ inches thick

½ cup freshly squeezed
lemon juice

1 green bell pepper, seeded
and cut into 1-inch squares

4 cherry tomatoes

I love swordfish. In fact, I love swordfish so much

that, the summer I was thirteen years old, I ate too much of it and didn't want to see it again for almost forty years. I only returned to swordfish a few summers back and now delight in cooking it. On the Vineyard, The Net Result in Vineyard Haven and Larsen's in Menemsha are my favorite fish markets. They sell the uneven bits of harpooned swordfish I use for this recipe at a special price. You may not find them at your fish store, but you can cut a swordfish steak to size.

Cut the swordfish into 1½-inch cubes. Place the cubes in a nonreactive bowl and sprinkle them with the lemon juice. Cover with plastic wrap and refrigerate for 1 hour.

When ready to cook, prepare a fire in a charcoal grill or preheat a gas grill. Oil the grill rack. Thread the swordfish pieces onto 4 skewers, dividing them evenly and alternating them with the bell pepper pieces. Top each skewer with a cherry tomato.

Place the skewers on the grill rack and cook for 2 to 3 minutes on each of the 4 sides of the swordfish cubes, or until lightly browned. Serve at once.

Kate Taylor's
White Clam Sauce

Kate Taylor is a member of the island's famous

Taylor family, whose members have enriched our musical lives for decades. She is also an artist, and collectors from all over seek her out for her wampum bracelets. When I put the call out for wampum beads, she was kind enough to unstring one of her own bracelets to provide the beads that were photographed to highlight the introduction of this book (see page 9) and bring them to my friend Mitzi Pratt's house. That's how we met. Before then, I'd only known her through one of her bracelets that I owned and through her musical appearances on the island.

Kate's kindness also extended to the promise of giving me her recipe for white clam sauce. Sure enough, when the time came, the recipe was delivered with complete instructions and a comment at the end that sums it all up: "Good eatin'." The sauce can be served over any type of pasta, but somehow seems to go best with linguine.

INGREDIENTS

1 pint shucked quahogs (see Sources, page 198) or other hard-shell clams

Bottled clam juice as needed

⅓ cup olive oil

4 cloves garlic, minced

1 bunch scallions, including 2 to 3 inches of green tops, sliced (about ½ cup)

½ cup chopped fresh parsley

½ teaspoon anchovy paste

3 tablespoons freshly squeezed lemon juice

1 pound linguine, cooked, drained, and piping hot

Freshly grated Parmesan cheese for serving

Drain the clams, reserving the liquid, and mince them. Measure the clam liquid and add bottled clam juice as needed to equal 2 cups. Set the minced meats and liquid aside separately.

Heat the olive oil in a heavy skillet over medium heat. Add the garlic and scallions and sauté gently for 2 minutes, or until translucent. Add the parsley and continue to sauté for another minute. Add the clam liquid and bring to a boil. Lower the heat and simmer for 3 minutes.

Add the clams to the skillet and heat slowly until hot, making sure that they do not boil. (You just want to bring them up to serving temperature.) Then add the anchovy paste and lemon juice and mix well.

Place the linguine in a warmed serving bowl and spoon the sauce over the pasta. Top with the cheese and serve immediately.

Arlen and Perry's
Mussels

SERVES 4

In the 1960s, after we'd had our house on the Vineyard for a few years, we met Arlen and Perry Westbrook, who became friends. They were bohemians from upstate New York and had a house right on Ocean Park in Oak Bluffs. Their Vineyard was different from ours and we tagged along occasionally and watched in delight as they did the Euell Gibbons thing, foraging for wild greens, ripe berries, and seafood that they would cook up and share with us. I remember one memorable occasion when we went out to Menemsha and returned with a bucket of mussels that we scrubbed and then steamed. It was unusual food in the days before bistros made *moules marinières* standard fare for many Americans. Serve the fragrant mussels with crusty bread.

Pick over the mussels, discarding any that fail to close to the touch and that are either too heavy or too light. The open ones are dead, the heavy ones are likely to contain only mud, and the light ones are probably dead or dying. Clean the mussels with a stiff brush, removing any barnacles and seaweed that are attached. Use a paring knife to remove any stubborn bits. Rinse the mussels in cool water. Finally, place the mussels in a large container with water to cover and allow them to sit for 2 to 3 hours to expel all sand. Drain and remove the beard (the hairlike filaments that the mussel uses to hold onto rocks or pilings) from each mussel by pulling it out.

Combine the wine, water, butter, onion, parsley sprigs, garlic, thyme, and a few grinds of pepper in an 8-quart pot. Place over medium heat, bring to a simmer, and simmer for 5 minutes. Add the mussels, cover, and raise the heat slightly. Allow the mussels to cook, stirring 2 or 3 times, for 4 to 5 minutes. They are ready when the shells open slightly and the bodies are plump. Be careful not to overcook the mussels.

Immediately divide the mussels evenly among 4 soup bowls, discarding any mussels that failed to open. Allow the broth to settle for a few minutes, so that any sand sinks to the bottom, then spoon the broth over the mussels. Top with the chopped parsley and serve.

INGREDIENTS

3 pounds mussels

1½ cups dry white wine

½ cup water

4 tablespoons butter

½ cup minced onion

4 sprigs fresh parsley

3 large cloves garlic, minced, or to taste

½ teaspoon dried thyme

Freshly ground black pepper to taste

½ cup chopped fresh parsley

Summer-Flavored Sea Bass

INGREDIENTS

1½ pounds sea bass fillet with skin intact, cut into 4 equal portions

4 tablespoons freshly squeezed lemon juice

3 tablespoons olive oil

2 cloves garlic, minced

½ cup minced garlic-stuffed olives

¼ cup minced sun-dried tomatoes

Sea bass is a seasonal favorite on the Vineyard,

and when my friend Tony Garnier returns from fishing with a piece for me, this is one of the ways I like to prepare it. The garlic, olives, lemon, and sun-dried tomatoes remind me of Provence and seem to bring the flavors of summer to the plate.

Place the sea bass fillet in a shallow platter and sprinkle with 2 tablespoons of the lemon juice, turning to coat both sides. Cover with plastic wrap and refrigerate for 1 hour.

When ready to cook, heat 2 tablespoons of the oil in a cast-iron skillet over medium-high heat. When the oil begins to smoke slightly, add the bass, skin-side down, and sear for 1 minute. Lower the heat to medium and cook for 5 to 6 minutes, then turn and cook on the other side for an additional 5 to 6 minutes, or until the fish flakes when tested with the tip of a knife. The cooking time will depend on the thickness of the fillet. Transfer the fish to a warmed platter.

Heat the remaining 1 tablespoon oil in the skillet over medium heat. Add the garlic, olives, and sun-dried tomatoes and stir to scrape up any browned bits. Add the remaining 2 tablespoons lemon juice and stir well to make sure the juice is warmed through. Pour the lemony sauce over the bass and serve immediately.

Mitzi's Bay Scallops
with Deep-Fried Kale

SERVES 4

Mitzi, an Aquinnah friend, is a bookbinder. I love

visiting her studio, where I purchase the hand-bound blank books that I use for my journals. Mitzi is also a gardener and a wonderful cook, and I usually return from my visits with a sack of fava beans, a few tomatoes, or other produce that she has grown. I also sometimes return with recipes like this one, which is great accompanied by white rice.

Rinse the kale well. Discard the stems and pick over and discard any discolored areas. Dry the leaves well with paper towels, then cut crosswise into narrow strips and set aside.

To make the sauce, combine the chile, oyster sauce, tamari, sherry, ginger, and garlic in a small bowl and stir to mix. Set aside.

Pour the oil to a depth of about 4 inches into a wok or deep cast-iron skillet and heat to 350°F on a deep-frying thermometer. When the oil is ready, add the kale and fry for 2 minutes, or until lightly crispy and slightly translucent. Using a slotted spoon, transfer to paper towels to drain.

Reheat the oil to 350°F. Add half of the scallops and fry for 2 to 3 minutes, or until opaque throughout and beginning to brown. Using the slotted spoon, transfer the scallops to paper towels to drain. Repeat with the remaining scallops.

Pour off all but 1 tablespoon of the oil from the pan and return the pan to medium heat. Add the sauce mixture and bring to a boil. Lower the heat, add the scallops, and stir-fry for 1 minute, or until heated through and the scallops are nicely coated with the sauce.

Transfer the scallops to a warmed serving plate and garnish with the kale. Serve immediately.

INGREDIENTS

6 ounces kale

1 fresh red chile, 2½ inches long, seeded and thinly sliced, or to taste

2 tablespoons oyster sauce

2 tablespoons tamari soy sauce

1 tablespoon dry sherry

1 tablespoon peeled and minced fresh ginger

1 tablespoon minced garlic

Peanut oil for frying

1 pound bay scallops (see Sources, page 198)

{ SCALLOPS }

Aequipecten irradians concentricus, or the Atlantic bay scallop, is one of my summer delights. Sure, these snowy shellfish are fine lightly sautéed and served up on a china plate, drizzled with a light beurre blanc, or slipped under a sauce for *coquilles Saint-Jacques.* But for me, the only way really to enjoy a bay scallop is when it is fried and I'm sitting in a spot where the wind tastes of the sea and the clanking of rigging against mast can be heard. My personal ritual is my first trip each year to the dockside spot known as Nancy's in Oak Bluffs, to sit under the thatched umbrellas and savor an order of fried scallops.

Small and sweet, the bay scallop is a bivalve that can grow up to three inches in diameter. The scallops thrive in shallow waters, usually where eelgrass provides the babies with nourishment in the form of larvae and with a wall of protection from predators. Every year my bay scallop treat is increasingly more difficult to find. They disappeared from Long Island over three decades ago and are becoming scarce on the Cape and Nantucket. The hope for their future may be on the Vineyard. We get a little scallop help from the Martha's Vineyard Shellfish Group, a thirty-plus-year-old organization that supplies juvenile shellfish to seed area ponds. The group has even worked with the Wampanoag to create a solar shellfish hatchery.

When scallop season opens on the Vineyard with a festive splash in mid-autumn, everyone heads to the ponds and gets their limit, and scallops take pride of place on local menus. I usually miss the celebrations, but I've had mine earlier, because with each bite of my annual scallop feast, I celebrate the reviving mollusk that is a part of the island's history and culture.

Roast Chicken

INGREDIENTS

1 frying chicken, 3½ to 4 pounds

3 tablespoons butter

2 tablespoons freshly squeezed lemon juice

1 onion

1 tablespoon Bell's poultry seasoning

Salt and freshly ground black pepper to taste

I love roast chicken. It's one of the few dishes that

I don't mind eating leftover the next day, so I'll cook a chicken for myself even if I'm dining solo. This recipe is as perfect for a Sunday dinner as it is for packing into a picnic hamper.

Preheat the oven to 450°F. Remove the bag of giblets from the cavity of the chicken and reserve for another use. Singe off any pinfeathers with a match. Rinse the bird inside and out and pat it dry.

Melt 1 tablespoon of the butter in a small saucepan over medium heat, then remove from the heat and set aside. Cut 1 tablespoon of the butter into small pieces. Using your fingers, gently loosen the skin on the breasts and legs of the chicken and insert the small pieces of butter between the skin and flesh, distributing them as evenly as possible. Pat the skin back into place.

Add the lemon juice to the melted butter and mix well. Rub the onion with the butter mixture, coating it evenly, then roll the onion in 1 teaspoon of the poultry seasoning, again coating evenly. Place the onion in the chicken cavity. Rub the exterior of the chicken with the remaining 1 tablespoon butter, 2 teaspoons poultry seasoning, and salt and pepper to taste.

Put the chicken, breast-side up, in a roasting pan. Place in the oven and roast for 15 minutes. Lower the heat to 350°F and continue to roast for 1 hour, or until the juices run clear when the thigh joint is pierced with a fork.

Remove from the oven and let rest for 10 minutes before carving and serving.

Curried Chicken Salad

SERVES 6 TO 8

The African American summer residents of Oak

Bluffs have brought their own brand of Southern gentility to the town's gingerbread cottages, and bridge and bid whist parties and ladies' lunches are still a favorite way to entertain friends. You might find this chicken salad at any one of them. It's simple and delicious and can make an elegant platter when surrounded by vine-ripened tomatoes, or by a mix of purple and green grapes—a smile at the Vineyard's name. Amid all of the fine ladies and elegant antique china, it seems almost churlish to tell you that the chicken salad is also a good way to get rid of the leftovers from last night's grilled chicken or Sunday's roasted one. You can serve the salad mounded on a platter or in pineapple wedges. If there's any salad left over, it makes a great sandwich spread for a picnic at the beach.

Combine the chicken, celery, onion, chutney, curry powder, and raisins in a bowl. Gradually add the mayonnaise, making sure that the salad is neither too wet nor too dry; each family has its preference. When you have reached the desired consistency, stop. Season with salt and pepper. Cover with plastic wrap and refrigerate for at least 1 hour so the flavors can blend.

Mound the chicken mixture on a platter and garnish with the tomatoes or grapes.

INGREDIENTS

5 cups chopped cooked chicken breast

1½ cups minced celery

1 tablespoon finely minced onion

1 tablespoon minced Major Grey's or other mango chutney

2 teaspoons hot Madras curry powder, or to taste

½ cup minced golden raisins

About ½ cup mayonnaise, freshly made or Hellmann's

Salt and freshly ground black pepper to taste

Sliced or quartered heirloom tomatoes or a mix of green and red grapes for garnish

Lemon-and-Thyme
Grilled Chicken Thighs

8 skin-on chicken thighs

⅓ cup dried thyme

¼ cup freshly squeezed lemon juice

2 tablespoons olive oil

I know it is supposed to be genteel to prefer white

meat chicken, but give me a leg or a thigh any day. I learned this recipe over thirty years ago from my late friend Kai Lofton. I love it as much now as I did then. The lemony flavor complements the juiciness of dark meat chicken, and the thyme adds a bit of crunch and loads of flavor. Because they are as good cold or at room temperature as they are hot, the thighs are good summer food, and you can even cut the meat off the bone and toss it in a salad for a fancy leftover dish. Those folks who eschew chicken skin will be pleased to know that this dish can be made with skinless chicken thighs, too, with only a little loss of taste.

Rinse the chicken thighs and place in a shallow nonreactive bowl. To make a marinade, combine the thyme, lemon juice, and olive oil in a small bowl and stir to mix. Pour the marinade over the chicken thighs, and then turn the thighs to ensure that each one is well coated with the liquid and evenly covered with thyme. Cover with plastic wrap, place in the refrigerator, and allow to marinate for at least 2 hours or for up to 4 hours.

When you're ready to cook, prepare a fire in a charcoal grill or preheat a gas grill or the broiler. Oil the grill rack. Remove the chicken pieces from the marinade, draining well. Place them on the grill rack, or on a broiler pan and slip under the broiler. Grill or broil, turning once, for about 10 minutes on each side, or until the chicken is browned and the juices run clear when a thigh is pierced with a fork. Serve hot, at room temperature, or cold.

Mommy's Summer Fried Chicken

SERVES 4 TO 6

This dish is a classic in the African American

repertoire. It's what my family ate on the road and on picnics and at home on Sundays. When it comes to fried chicken, there are two basic types of cooks: the dredgers and the batterers. I'm a dredger, preferring the crunch of a crisp skin that is free of batter. This is my mother's recipe. The Bell's poultry seasoning is not optional, as other brands will have a different taste.

1 frying chicken, 2 ½ to 3 pounds, cut into serving pieces

Vegetable oil for frying

½ cup flour

¼ cup white cornmeal

1½ tablespoons Bell's poultry seasoning

1 teaspoon salt

½ teaspoon freshly ground black pepper

Rinse the chicken pieces and pat dry with paper towels. Pour the oil to a depth of about 2 inches into a deep cast-iron skillet and heat to 350°F on a deep-frying thermometer. While the oil is heating, combine the flour, cornmeal, poultry seasoning, salt, and pepper in a brown paper bag and shake to mix well. Place the chicken pieces, a few at a time, in the bag and shake well to coat evenly. Remove from the bag and shake off the excess flour mixture.

Working in batches, place the chicken pieces in the skillet and fry, turning the pieces as they brown, for 15 to 20 minutes, or until crispy and cooked through. To check for doneness, prick the pieces with a fork in the thickest part; the juices should run clear with no trace of blood. Transfer to paper towels to drain and keep warm in a low oven. Repeat with the remaining chicken pieces. Serve hot, warm, or at room temperature.

NOTE: The chicken is traditionally drained on pieces of brown paper bag, but paper towels will do just fine.

{ FARM STANDS }

A map has been compiled, but I prefer the surprise of discovering the island's farm stands as I ride around. And I always keep some small bills ready to spend, because I make my friends brake for farm stands. The stands dot the island like mushrooms, springing up when there is a bumper crop and then disappearing until another season. Most folks' summers are punctuated by these small places off the side of the road, where a table laden with large tomato juice cans filled with zinnias and cosmos and a pile of tomatoes and corn brings traffic to a halt. They turn in, step out, and do a bit of island-style shopping.

There are the well-known farm stands, like Norton and Morning Glory, that attract buyers year after year with large signs and a seasonal array of goods that ranges from the first corn of the season to the freshest salad greens. They've grown over the years into weathered outbuildings complete with cash registers and people in attendance to weigh and bag. These are standbys for the folks who want their produce fresh daily and can't always wait for the biweekly farmers' market.

Then, there are the smaller spots where a card table or venerable kitchen standby holds a few items: carrots that have dirt still clinging to them, bunches of flowers roughly tied with twine, and the tomatoes that are the leitmotif of most summer salads. Here, there are no attendants, and the honor system—a cigar box for cash and change—reigns supreme in a throwback to the Vineyard of yore.

There are even smaller, quirkier spots, like the blue-and-white cooler on a bench in front of Bittersweet, an up-island restaurant. The cognoscenti scramble to reach it, knowing that it holds a mix of fresh and wild greens specially prepared by the chef.

No matter the size of the stand or the nature of the foods sold, these locations are living witness to the diligence of the local farmers whose bounty supported the island population for years. Even now, they produce so much that no visitor need leave the island without sampling a taste of its wares.

Jagacida

2 tablespoons olive oil

1 small onion, minced

¾ cup minced linguiça

2 teaspoons minced garlic

¼ cup sweet paprika

3 cups water

2 bay leaves

Salt and freshly ground
black pepper to taste

1 can (16 ounces) butter
beans, undrained

1 cup long-grain white rice,
preferably Uncle Ben's

The Cape Verdeans have been on Martha's Vineyard

for centuries. Able fishermen, they were among those who went out on the whaling ships commanded by Edgartown sea captains. Their bravery at sea is legendary; their prowess in the kitchen is less well known, but no less awesome. They've given us the hearty, quick meal known affectionately as "jag." The trick with jag is to get the right consistency. A Cape Verdean tests it by standing a teaspoon in the middle of the pot. If it falls too easily, there's too much water; if it stands firm, there's not enough. Use your own judgment. This recipe was given to me by Carleen Cordwell, a New Bedford native who spends time on the Vineyard.

Heat the olive oil in a heavy saucepan over medium heat. Add the onion and linguiça and sauté for about 2 minutes, or until the sausage has rendered some of its fat. Add the garlic and paprika and continue to cook, stirring, for 3 minutes, or until the sausage is heated through and the onion is translucent but not brown.

Add the water and bay leaves, season with a little salt and pepper, cover, and bring to a boil.

Add the beans and their liquid and the rice and stir to make sure that all of the ingredients are well mixed. Cover, reduce the heat to low, and cook for about 30 minutes, or until the rice is tender.

Remove and discard the bay leaves. Taste and adjust the seasoning with the salt and pepper. Serve hot.

Hot Dogs,
Plain and Fancy

SERVES 4

Sure, they're super-simple and we all know how to

make them, but hot dogs are a classic summer food. I find that even on days when the clouds cover the sun and the beach seems a distant memory, these hot dogs, plain or fancy depending on my whimsy, are just the thing to bring summer right back. The trick is to obtain crustless New England frankfurter rolls. They are what allow you to toast the outsides for the special summer-at-the-shore taste.

Prepare a fire in a charcoal grill or preheat a gas grill.

To make the plain dogs: Place 4 of the hot dogs on the grill rack and grill, turning often, for 6 to 8 minutes, or until they show grill marks on the exterior and are hot throughout. Toast 4 of the rolls on the grill and slip a hot dog into each roll.

To make the fancy dogs: Make a lengthwise slit in each of the remaining 4 hot dogs. Place the cheese strips in the slits. Wrap each hot dog in a bacon strip, securing the ends in place with toothpicks. Place the hot dogs on the grill rack and grill, turning often, for 6 to 8 minutes, or until the bacon is crisp, the cheese is melted, and the dogs are hot throughout. Toast the remaining 4 rolls on the grill and slip a hot dog into each roll.

Serve the hot dogs immediately, giving each person 1 plain and 1 fancy. Accompany the plain dogs with the mustard and relish and the fancy dogs with the mustard, relish, and chutney.

INGREDIENTS

8 hot dogs

8 New England frankfurter rolls (see Sources, page 198)

½ pound sharp Vermont Cheddar cheese, cut into thin, narrow strips

4 strips bacon

Dijon mustard for serving

Hot dog relish for serving

½ cup tomato chutney, homemade (page 69) or purchased

Outside-In
Blue Cheese Burgers

¼ pound blue cheese

1 pound ground chuck

4 hamburger rolls, split

Condiments as desired
for serving

I'm a blue-cheese lover. From Roquefort dressing

to a crumble in a Cobb salad to a sliver or two eaten atop a slice of crisp chilled pear, there's nothing like it. Here, I've turned a cheeseburger inside-out, burying the blue cheese in the middle, where it waits as a surprise for the diner.

With a melon baller, scoop the blue cheese into 4 equal rounds. Enclose the rounds in waxed paper, and place in the freezer for 1 hour.

When you're ready to cook the burgers, prepare a fire in a charcoal grill or preheat a gas grill. Oil the grill rack. Divide the meat into 4 equal portions and shape each portion into a thick patty, encasing 1 cheese round in the middle of each patty.

Place the patties on the grill rack and grill, turning once, until cooked to desired doneness. Just before the burgers are ready, toast the hamburger rolls on the grill.

Serve the burgers hot on the toasted rolls with the condiments.

Peppercorn-Crusted Steak
with Roquefort Sauce

More blue cheese, more beef. This is the adult version of Outside-In Blue Cheese Burgers (page 112), with a Roquefort sauce for spooning over porterhouse steak.

Prepare a fire in a charcoal grill or preheat a gas grill. Oil the grill rack. Trim excess fat from the steak and pat the steak dry with paper towels. Place the sea salt, peppercorns, thyme, *herbes de Provence*, and ground chile in a spice grinder and pulse until you have a coarse powder. Rub the powder into both sides of the steak.

Place the steak on the grill rack and grill, turning once, until cooked to desired doneness.

Make the sauce. While the steak is cooking, place the yogurt and blue cheese in a small bowl. Whisking constantly, slowly drizzle in the milk, continuing to whisk until you have a thick sauce that is not too runny.

Cut the steak into 4 equal portions and place on individual plates. Serve immediately with the sauce.

INGREDIENTS

1 porterhouse steak, about 2 pounds and 1½ inches thick

2 tablespoons sea salt

2 tablespoons mixed peppercorns

1 tablespoon dried thyme

1 tablespoon *herbes de Provence*

¼ teaspoon ground chipotle chile

ROQUEFORT SAUCE

1½ tablespoons plain yogurt

1 tablespoon crumbled Roquefort or other blue cheese

1 tablespoon milk

Lavender, Garlic, and Rosemary
Leg of Lamb
with Spicy Mint Sauce

1 shank end half, bone-in leg of lamb, 4 to 5 pounds

6 large cloves garlic

1½ teaspoons dried lavender buds

1 tablespoon fresh thyme leaves

2 tablespoons sea salt

2 tablespoons mixed peppercorns

1 tablespoon dried rosemary

1 tablespoon *herbes de Provence*

SPICY MINT SAUCE

1 jar (8 ounces) mint jelly

1 small jalapeño chile, seeded and minced, or to taste

2 tablespoons dark rum

Once or twice during the summer, I give up my

meals of simple grilled meats and fish, buy a big roast, and have friends over for a more formal dinner. When that happens, among my favorite dishes to serve is roast leg of lamb. One of the things that I like about lamb is that it is a meat I enjoy at all stages of doneness, so I am not averse to serving it medium, in order to please my friends who don't like rare meat. My garden has a lavender bed and a few rosemary plants, so I head out there and collect two of the three ingredients that give this lamb its particular flavor; then I get cooking.

The mint sauce is a quick way to add a bit of heat and flavor to traditional mint jelly.

Preheat the oven to 450°F. If the butcher has not already removed the fell (parchmentlike membrane) from the lamb leg, trim it away along with all excess fat. Using the tip of a sharp knife, make 15 or so small incisions in the leg, spacing them evenly. Place the garlic, lavender, and fresh thyme in a small food processor and pulse until you have a thick paste. Slip a bit of the paste into each of the incisions in the lamb. Place the sea salt, peppercorns, dried rosemary, and *herbes de Provence* in a spice grinder and pulse until you have a coarse mix. Rub the mix all over the lamb, covering it evenly. Place a rack in a roasting pan, and place the lamb on the rack.

Roast the lamb for 15 minutes. Lower the heat to 350°F and continue to roast for about 1 hour, or until a thermometer inserted into the thickest part away from bone registers 130°F for rare, 140° to 145°F for medium-rare, or 160°F for well-done. Cooking times will vary depending on the shape of the lamb and the consistent heat of your oven. Remove the lamb from the oven and let rest for 15 minutes before carving.

Make the mint sauce. While the lamb is resting, combine the mint jelly, chile, and rum in a small saucepan over medium heat. Cook, stirring occasionally, for about 5 minutes, or until the jelly liquefies and the sauce is warmed through.

Carve the lamb parallel to the bone in long, thin slices and arrange the slices on a platter. Transfer the warm sauce to a sauceboat and pass at the table.

Vegetables

{ VEGETABLES }

132
Stir-Fried Broccoli with Sun-Dried Tomatoes and Garlic

135
Baby French Beans

136
Spinach with Soy and Lemon

137
Baked Potatoes with Pimentón Yogurt

138
Carrots in Passionfruit and Orange Juices

141
Summer Southern Succotash

143
Marvino's Lobster Grits

144
Suesan's Corn Bread–Collard Green Pie

145
Home-Style Corn Bread

Aquinnah

Like many longtime residents of the Vineyard,

I have a hard time remembering to call the westernmost point of the island Aquinnah, the Wampanoag name it returned to in 1998. It is the island's smallest community, but it is undoubtedly the one with the longest history, for the Wampanoag were on the island when the European settlers arrived. I often find myself still calling it Gay Head, as the town was known in my youth, an homage to the multicolored cliffs that astonish with their vibrant colors and their views. In those days, the cliffs were open to the public, and I vividly remember descending them with my grandmother. I also recall annual visits to the souvenir shop at the edge of the cliffs, where Napoleon Madison held forth and kept traditions alive. The shop made a wicked clam chowder that my father adored, and a buttery toasted frankfurter on a New England roll that was my childhood delight.

The shop is still there, along with others that have sprung up on the way to the cliffs. The food is still memorable as well, with the traditional chowders and hot dogs vying with newer wraps and veggie burgers. Somehow the food of Aquinnah just seems to have an extra tasty je ne sais quoi. Perhaps it's because it was the Wampanoag who first farmed and fished on the Vineyard. Their descendants still retain their respect for the land, as evidenced in the celebration of Cranberry Day in October and in their honoring of tradition in the annual Moshup Pageant in late summer, which celebrates the island's benevolent patron giant.

Corn Pudding

3 eggs

2 cups freshly cut corn kernels

¼ cup flour

1 teaspoon salt

½ teaspoon freshly ground white pepper

2 tablespoons butter, melted

2 cups heavy cream

Corn, beans, and squashes were known by the

island's first residents as the Three Sisters, because they were cultivated in symbiotic sorority. The beans climbed on the trellis provided by the cornstalks; the leaves of the squashes offered ground cover and protection from insects. When served together, they provided a balanced diet. No one knows exactly when corn arrived on the island, but the Wampanoag revered it and cultivated it, burying the seed corn in mounds, fertilizing the young plants with fish heads, and carefully tending the stalks as they grew. By 1631, corn was so important in the Massachusetts Bay Colony that it was made legal tender. It's not surprising, therefore, that when corn is in season, it takes pride of place on the table. This corn pudding is one of the many ways in which it appears.

Preheat the oven to 325°F. Beat the eggs in a bowl until foamy. Add the corn, flour, salt, and pepper and stir well. Then add the butter and cream and again stir to mix. Pour the mixture into a 1½-quart baking dish. Place the baking dish in a larger baking pan or roasting pan, and add hot water to the pan to reach halfway up the sides of the baking dish, to create a bain-marie.

Bake the pudding uncovered for 1 hour, or until a knife inserted into the center comes out dry. Serve hot.

Ratatouille

Summer brings a bounty of vegetables to Martha's

Vineyard, which paints the farmers' market in bright Van Gogh hues of crimson, orange, and aubergine. This dish is one of the ways to bring those colors to the summer table. It's good served hot or at room temperature.

Heat the olive oil in a large skillet over medium heat. Add the onion and sauté for 3 to 5 minutes, or until translucent. Add the bell peppers and eggplant and continue to cook, stirring occasionally, for 5 minutes. Add the zucchini and tomatoes, reduce the heat to low, cover, and simmer for about 10 minutes, or until all the vegetables are tender.

Add the parsley, oregano, basil, and garlic and season with salt and pepper. Stir to mix well and continue to cook, uncovered, for 10 minutes longer to blend the flavors. Serve hot, at room temperature, or chilled.

INGREDIENTS

6 tablespoons olive oil

1 large onion, sliced

1 green bell pepper, seeded and diced

1 yellow bell pepper, seeded and diced

1 eggplant, trimmed and cubed

2 zucchini, trimmed and cubed

5 ripe tomatoes, peeled, seeded, and chopped

1 tablespoon minced fresh flat-leaf parsley

⅛ teaspoon dried Italian oregano

½ teaspoon dried basil

1 large clove garlic, minced

Salt and freshly ground black pepper to taste

Corn
Fritters

When the corn is fresh on the Vineyard I want to

eat it on the cob, but after it sits for a day or two, I like it in a variety of different ways. These corn fritters, one of my favorite recipes, may be served almost any time of the day from breakfast through dinner. In a pinch, they may even be dusted with powdered sugar and do duty as dessert.

Pour the oil to a depth of about 3 inches into a deep, heavy skillet and heat the oil to 375°F on a deep-frying thermometer. While the oil is heating, break the eggs into a bowl. Whisk the eggs while drizzling in the milk. Add the flour, baking powder, salt, and melted butter. Finally, stir in the corn.

When the oil is ready, drop the batter by the spoonful into the hot oil, being careful not to crowd the pan. Fry for about 2 minutes, or until golden brown. Using a slotted spoon, transfer to paper towels to drain. Repeat with the remaining batter. Keep each batch hot in a low oven until all the fritters are cooked, then serve immediately.

INGREDIENTS

Vegetable oil for frying

2 eggs

½ cup milk

1 cup sifted flour

1 teaspoon baking powder

½ teaspoon salt

1 teaspoon butter, melted

1½ cups cooked freshly cut corn kernels

Milk-and-Honey Corn
with Two Butters

INGREDIENTS

6 ears corn, shucked

Lime-Cayenne Butter and/or
Jalapeño Butter (following)

LIME-CAYENNE BUTTER

3 tablespoons butter,
at room temperature

2 teaspoons olive oil

⅛ teaspoon freshly grated
lime zest

Pinch of cayenne pepper,
or to taste

JALAPEÑO BUTTER

1 jalapeño chile, minced,
or to taste

4 tablespoons butter,
at room temperature

¼ teaspoon minced
fresh cilantro

When the corn is fresh in the markets in Martha's

Vineyard, I eat it daily. Sometimes I'll just remove the silk and microwave it in the husk for a few minutes. Sometimes I'll boil it, and sometimes I'll roast it on the grill, which reminds me of the roasted-corn vendors that I haunt in the Caribbean and West Africa. This is the roasted version, complete with two butters for slathering.

Prepare a fire in a charcoal grill or preheat a gas grill or broiler. Oil the grill rack or the broiler-pan rack. Place the corn on the grill rack, or on the broiler pan and slip under the broiler. Grill or broil, turning the ears frequently, for 5 to 7 minutes, or until the corn is lightly charred in spots.

Serve the corn hot with one or both of the butters on the side for slathering.

To make each butter recipe, combine all of the ingredients in a small bowl and mix until well blended. Cover with plastic wrap and chill for 1 hour before serving.

Brazilian Greens

Traditionally, this dish is called *couve* and accompanies

Brazil's national dish, *feijoada*, a rich stew of black beans and mixed meats. It is usually prepared with kale, but it is also good made with the collard greens that are emblematic of the African American table. Collards cooked this way are a quicker and healthier alternative to the traditional Southern method for cooking greens.

Rinse the greens thoroughly. Stack some of the leaves, tightly roll up the stack lengthwise, and cut crosswise into narrow strips. (This is called chiffonade, a classic French technique.) Repeat with the remaining leaves.

Heat the olive oil in a large, heavy skillet over medium heat. Add the garlic and cook, stirring, for 2 to 3 minutes, or until only lightly browned. Add the collards and cook, stirring constantly, for 5 minutes, or until the greens are soft but still bright green. Add the water, cover, reduce the heat to low, and continue to cook for 2 minutes, or until the greens wilt slightly.

Serve the greens immediately. Pass the hot sauce at the table.

INGREDIENTS

2 pounds young collard greens

3 tablespoons olive oil

8 cloves garlic, minced, or to taste

1 tablespoon water

Brazilian Hot Sauce (page 74) or hot sauce of choice

{ MOSHUP'S TABLE }

The Wampanoag called the part of the island on which they lived *Aquinnah*, "meadow under the hill," or *Kuhtuhquehtuet*, "place of rising ground." Both descriptions still apply today to the area that the English called Gay Head. The Indians greeted the English interlopers with gifts of tobacco, deer skins, and cooked fish, and John Brereton, one of the men in Bartholomew Gosnold's 1602 expedition to the island, described them as "tall, big-boned men" and reckoned them friendly.

Early European accounts of the island stress its abundance and spend time talking about the local strawberries that the would-be colonizers found tastier than the ones at home. Sassafras was also plentiful, and was much sought after as a cure for syphilis. The treasures of the sea—scallops, mussels, clams, cockles, crabs, oysters, and more—amazed the explorers not only by their profusion, but also by their size.

Gardens were well tended, with corn grown in symbiosis with beans and squashes as elsewhere in the hemisphere. Corn was called *weatchimin* and was central to the diet. It was most often eaten in the form of samp or newsamp, a porridge similar to the large hominy of the South or to Mexico's *posole*. Animal protein came not only from fish, but also from other creatures, ranging from deer to skunk, but carnivore flesh was generally avoided. It was an essentially healthful diet with ample grains, limited but sufficient animal protein, and seasonal fresh fruits and vegetables.

Cranberries, acorns, raspberries, and wild cherries all turned up in the gourds and fired-clay ceramic dishes used as eating utensils. Vegetables and herbs also were found in abundance and were used not only for food, but also for medicinal purposes. Wintergreen was taken for pain relief, raspberry root for sore throats, and dogwood bark for colds.

In times of celebration, there were clambakes featuring corn on the cob, lobsters, oysters, and clams. You'll see similar get-togethers today on the beaches under the brightly colored cliffs that have gazed down on generations of Wampanoag and tourists alike as they savored the bounty of Moshup, the legendary giant patron of the land.

Stir-Fried Broccoli
with Sun-Dried Tomatoes and Garlic

1 head broccoli, about
¾ pound

1½ tablespoons olive oil

4 large cloves garlic, slivered

2 tablespoons finely snipped
sun-dried tomato

Salt and freshly ground black
pepper to taste

Broccoli is a standby for me. It's available year-round,

so it comes to the table in many guises. My favorite way to prepare it is to stir-fry it with garlic. Once, when the late Bernice Slaughter, an island friend, was ailing, I took her a meal that included broccoli. I wanted to doll it up a bit for the woman whom I called the Empress of Oak Bluffs, so I added snippets of sun-dried tomato for color. I liked them so well that now I always add them.

Break or cut off the florets from the broccoli head. Peel the stalks and cut them into ¹/₂-inch pieces. Bring a 3-quart saucepan filled with water to a rolling boil. Drop in the broccoli and parboil for 3 minutes. Drain the broccoli, then immediately "shock" it by dropping it into a bowl of ice water to stop the cooking. Drain again and pat dry.

Heat the olive oil in a wok or heavy skillet over medium heat. Add the garlic slivers and cook them rapidly, stirring constantly, for 1 minute. Add the sun-dried tomato and broccoli and continue to cook, stirring, for an additional 2 to 3 minutes, or until the broccoli is fork-tender but still crunchy. Season with salt and pepper and serve immediately.

Baby French Beans

When I can find them on the island, the small,

slender string beans known as haricots verts are one of my favorite vegetables. When I can't find them, I look for the freshest, smallest string beans and cook them the same way.

Bring a 3-quart saucepan filled with water to a rolling boil. Drop in the beans and parboil for 3 minutes. Drain the beans, then immediately "shock" them by dropping them into a bowl of ice water to stop the cooking. Drain again and pat dry.

Heat the butter in a skillet over medium heat until foaming. Add the garlic and cook, stirring constantly, for 1 minute, or until fragrant. Add the beans and continue to cook, stirring constantly, for 1 minute longer, or until the garlic is lightly browned and the beans are just tender. Serve immediately.

INGREDIENTS

1 pound haricots verts or young, small string beans, stem ends trimmed

2 tablespoons butter

2 cloves garlic, minced

Spinach *with* Soy and Lemon

2 pounds spinach

2 tablespoons water

1 tablespoon low-sodium soy sauce

1 tablespoon freshly squeezed lemon juice

I discovered this mix of tastes at Japanese restaurants.

I serve the spinach warm or slightly chilled as a salad.

Rinse the spinach well. Place in a saucepan, add the water, cover, and place over medium heat. Cook, stirring occasionally for even cooking, for 3 minutes, or until the spinach is wilted and the water has evaporated. Drain well.

Transfer the spinach to a serving bowl. Mix the soy sauce and lemon juice together in a small bowl, and pour it over the spinach. Serve warm, or let cool, chill slightly, and serve as a salad.

Baked Potatoes
with Pimentón Yogurt

SERVES 4

Potatoes can be cooked on an outdoor grill, much

the same way they are cooked in an oven. I slather mine with a thin coating of olive oil and then place them in aluminum foil. You can cut calories by skipping the usual addition of sour cream at the table and substituting yogurt seasoned with the smoked Spanish paprika known as *pimentón* in its place.

Prepare a fire in a charcoal grill or preheat a gas grill. Scrub the potatoes and prick them with a fork. Slather the potatoes with the olive oil and enclose each potato in a foil packet, sealing securely. Place the foil packets on the grill rack and grill, turning them occasionally, for 1 hour, or until the potatoes are easily pricked with a fork.

While the potatoes are cooking, make the yogurt topping. Combine the yogurt, scallions, and *pimentón* in a small bowl and mix well.

When the potatoes are ready, remove them from their packets and place on individual plates. Diners slit them open with a knife and add the *pimentón* yogurt to taste.

INGREDIENTS

4 medium-sized Yukon Gold potatoes

2 tablespoons olive oil

½ cup plain yogurt

2 scallions, including 2 inches of green tops, chopped

¼ teaspoon hot *pimentón*

Carrots in Passionfruit
and Orange Juices

INGREDIENTS

6 carrots, peeled and cut into ½-inch-thick slices (about 2 cups)

½ cup passionfruit juice

½ cup freshly squeezed orange juice

Salt and freshly ground black pepper to taste

Ground ginger for dusting

1 sprig fresh mint

Carrots fresh out of the dirt have a sweetness all

their own, which is enhanced by cooking them in a mix of passionfruit and orange juices. No one can ever quite guess what juices have been used, but everyone agrees that the carrots are delicious.

Place the carrots and both juices in a saucepan and season with salt and pepper. Bring to a boil over high heat. Lower the heat to a simmer and cook, uncovered, for 10 minutes, or until the carrots are fork-tender.

Remove from the heat, drain, and place in a serving bowl. Dust with the ginger, top with the mint sprig, and serve.

NOTE: When you drain the carrots, you can discard the cooking liquid, or you can save it, chill it, and drink it at another time.

Summer Southern Succotash

For many, succotash is the classic Native American

dish of corn and lima beans, but for Southerners, it is a mix of okra, corn, and tomatoes. This dish is never finer than during the summer months when all of the ingredients are just coming into their prime. On the Vineyard, where okra can be found only occasionally, this succotash is a real treat. When the okra is fresh, it is wonderful with the sweet-tart character of summer tomatoes and the sun-generated sugar of just-picked corn. The habanero chile adds just enough kick. Chile-heads will want to keep it in a bit longer, while those with more delicate taste buds may want to leave it out entirely.

Combine all of the ingredients except the salt and pepper in a saucepan, stir to mix, and place over medium heat. Bring to a boil, lower the heat to a simmer, cover, and cook for 15 minutes, or until the vegetables are tender and the flavors are well blended. If you used the chile, remove it from the pan when the dish has reached the desired spiciness. Season with salt and pepper and serve hot.

INGREDIENTS

6 large, ripe tomatoes, peeled, seeded, and coarsely chopped

2 cups freshly cut corn kernels

1 pound okra, tops and tails trimmed and cut into ½-inch-thick rounds

1 habanero chile, pricked with a fork (optional)

1½ cups water

Salt and freshly ground black pepper to taste

Marvino's Lobster Grits

Marvin Jones has long since closed Lobster in the Bluffs, his much beloved restaurant in Oak Bluffs, but he remains one of the island's caterers and is a master of invention. He came up with this dish to use the seafood-rich broth left over from his one-pot shore dinner (page 87), but any good seafood stock will do. It is a wonderful breakfast or brunch treat and approaches the sublime when you use the speckled white grits made from whole-grain unbolted heirloom dent corn sold by my buddy Hoppin' John Taylor.

INGREDIENTS

4 cups seafood broth

2 tablespoons butter

Salt to taste

1 cup whole-grain grits (see Sources, page 198)

1 pound cooked lobster tail meat

Combine the broth, butter, and salt in a 5-quart saucepan and bring to a rolling boil. Gradually add the grits, stirring constantly, and let the mixture return to a boil. Lower the heat to a simmer and cook the grits uncovered, stirring occasionally so that they do not stick or form a skin, for about 25 minutes, or until they are creamy or done to your taste. Folks who like to cook their grits longer will need more liquid.

When the grits are done, spoon them into individual bowls and top each bowl with one-fourth of the lobster. Serve immediately.

Suesan's Corn Bread–
Collard Green Pie

Home-Style Corn Bread
batter (facing page)

½ cup (1 stick) butter, at
room temperature

½ pound yellow summer
squashes, trimmed and
coarsely chopped

Salt to taste

2 tablespoons olive oil

4 onions, chopped

5 cloves garlic, minced

1 pound fresh collard greens,
rinsed, stems discarded, and
leaves torn into small pieces

Low-sodium soy sauce
to taste

½ teaspoon dried thyme,
or to taste

Freshly ground black
pepper to taste

Suesan Stovall is an Oak Bluffs summer resident

whom the gods have blessed abundantly with talent. She's a magnificent singer whose island performances are all too rare, and the annual showing of her spiritually based collages and assemblages is one of the high points of the late-summer season, attracting up-island and down-island residents who mix, mingle, and fight over who will buy which works. On top of all that, she's a great cook and often whips up a collation for the opening of her art show. This corn bread–collard green pie is one of her specialties and pulls out all of the Southern–African American culinary stops. Serve with a green salad

Preheat the oven to 400°F. Prepare the corn bread batter as directed and reserve. Put 4 tablespoons of the butter in a 9-by-12-inch baking pan and place in the oven. When the butter has melted, remove the pan from the oven and reserve.

Place the squashes in a saucepan and add salted water to cover. Bring to a boil and boil for 8 minutes, or until the squash is soft. Drain well and place in a bowl. Season with salt and then mash in the remaining 4 tablespoons butter with a fork. Set aside.

Heat the olive oil in a skillet over medium heat. Add the onions and garlic and sauté for 2 to 3 minutes, or until the onions are lightly browned. Add the collard greens, season with the soy sauce, thyme, and pepper, and continue to cook, stirring occasionally from the bottom so the onions don't stick, for 6 to 7 minutes, or until the greens are wilted. Remove from the heat.

Pour half of the corn bread batter into the butter in the baking pan. Spoon the collard greens mixture on top of the batter. Spread the squash mixture on top of the greens, and cover with the remaining batter. Bake for 20 minutes, or until golden brown. Remove from the oven and let cool. Cut into squares to serve.

Home-Style
Corn Bread

This is Suesan Stovall's corn bread, the one she

uses for her corn bread–collard green pie (facing page). I stand firmly on the side of those who think that any more than a pinch of sugar in the batter is anathema, but this corn bread and its hint of sweetness enhances the pie.

Preheat the oven to 400°F. Place the butter in a 9-by-12-inch baking pan and place in the oven. (If you're using the corn bread batter to make the pie, follow the directions for melting butter in the pie recipe; you'll need to melt only half the amount indicated here.) When the butter has melted, remove the pan from the oven and reserve.

Combine the cornmeal, flour, sugar, baking powder, salt, eggs, and milk in a bowl and stir until a smooth batter forms. Pour the batter into the butter in the baking pan. Bake for 20 minutes, or until golden on top. Remove from the oven, let cool, and cut into squares to serve.

INGREDIENTS

½ cup (1 stick) butter

1 cup yellow cornmeal

1 cup flour

¼ cup sugar

1 tablespoon baking powder

1 teaspoon salt

2 eggs

1 cup milk

Desserts

{ DESSERTS }

Edgartown

Sea captains' white houses with widow's walks, roses tumbling over picket fences, and lush green lawns characterize Edgartown in the summer. This is the county seat for Duke's County, home to the island's courthouse and its county jail (also in one of those white clapboard houses!). In times past, Edgartown's fame came from the wealth of its sea captains, and even today the town is marked by a sense of the comfort of the past and present coming together.

Edgartown is the most preppy of the island's towns, so visitors are likely to see blue blazers, khakis, and pants sporting all manner of spouting whales. But the town also has its more relaxed side: beaches, farms, and miles of dunes. Visitors can head to the beaches of Katama Bay, where rough surf pounds ashore, or to South Beach, where the young set frolics. Then there is Chappaquiddick, or Chappy as it is affectionately known, where fishermen and -women go out to surf cast for striped bass and bluefish in the waters off Wasque. As Kennedy lore fades, Chappy is now known for the Mytoi Japanese Garden and Wildlife Preserve and for the astonishingly brief ride on the two-car flatboat ferry, *On Time*, to get there.

As one of the two "wet" towns on the island, Edgartown is also site of an active nightlife and features all kinds of restaurants, from grab-it-and-run joints offering fried clams and sushi to such sophisticated dining spots as Alchemy, Atria, and L'Etoile.

Blueberry Grunt

My neighbor Barb Peckham is a superb cook with

a stock of old Yankee recipes from family members. She gave me this recipe for a classic New England dessert with the following note: "As I understand it, a grunt, also called a slump in northern New England, was made with dumplings, as opposed to biscuit or pie crust, so that it could be cooked in a tight-lidded pot over the fire and would not have to be baked in an oven. Originally, this would have been used as a breakfast dish. Much later, it came to be used as dessert."

Combine the sugar, salt, and cornstarch in a large nonreactive saucepan with a tight-fitting lid and stir to mix. Add the lemon juice and water and bring the mixture to a boil over medium-high heat, stirring constantly until it thickens slightly and is smooth. Add the berries and cook for 2 to 3 minutes longer. Remove from the heat and set the pan aside while you prepare the dumplings.

Make the dumplings. Combine the flour, baking powder, salt, and sugar in a bowl and stir to mix. Add the milk and blend it in with a fork. Scrape down the bowl sides with a rubber spatula.

Finish the grunt by bringing the blueberry mixture back to a boil. Drop the dumpling batter by large spoonfuls evenly onto the surface of the bubbling mixture, making 4 to 6 dumplings, and then cover tightly. Reduce the heat to low and cook without uncovering for 12 minutes. The dumplings will have risen and be dry in the center.

To serve, put a dumpling in each dessert dish and spoon the blueberry mixture over it. Serve with the ice cream or whipped cream.

INGREDIENTS

1 cup sugar

Pinch of salt

1 tablespoon cornstarch

Juice of 1 lemon (about 1½ tablespoons)

1½ cups plus 2 tablespoons water

4 to 4 ½ cups blueberries

DUMPLINGS

1½ cups flour

3½ teaspoons baking powder

½ teaspoon salt

1 scant tablespoon sugar

¾ cup milk

Vanilla ice cream or whipped cream for topping

Lavender Cookies

INGREDIENTS

¾ cup (1½ sticks) unsalted butter

¼ cup superfine sugar, plus more for sprinkling

1 tablespoon dried lavender buds

1½ cups flour

I can't pinpoint exactly when it happened, but one summer not long ago Oak Bluffs discovered lavender. It flourishes in the sandy soil that is our gardening lot. Soon bees were buzzing contentedly in the lavender patch outside of the post office, and bushes flourished along some of the walkways on Circuit Avenue. I got into the mood, planted some, and made lavender sachets until my drawers were filled with the fresh scent of lavender. I then turned to lavender's culinary uses and begged Mary Len Costa, a New Orleans friend, for her recipe for lavender cookies, which she regularly bakes and sends to friends. This is it. The cookies pair well with a summer sorbet or are a good addition to a tea table.

Preheat the oven to 400°F. Butter a cookie sheet.

Combine the butter and ¼ cup sugar in a bowl. Using an electric mixer or wooden spoon, beat together until fluffy. Add the lavender and flour and mix until you have a dough that holds its shape.

On a floured work surface, roll out the dough about ¼ inch thick. Cut out the cookies with a 2-inch round fluted cookie cutter (Mary Len usually makes hearts). Arrange the cutouts on the prepared cookie sheet.

Bake for 12 to 14 minutes, or until golden. Transfer the cookies to a rack and allow them to cool completely. Sprinkle them with superfine sugar and serve. Store any leftover cookies in an airtight container at room temperature for up to 3 weeks.

Tipsy Watermelon

I call my house in Oak Bluffs my "watermelon house."

I have paintings of the fruit by various artist friends, and the kitchen is decorated with examples of what a friend has dubbed "watermelonania." For years, I could take or leave watermelon, preferring the sweet-tart taste of watermelon rind pickles and not really wanting the summer's special fruit. Then one day, I'm not sure why, I found myself craving watermelon, loving it when it is at its summer sweetest, and even buying it from fruit stands in the cooler months.

This recipe is almost too simple, requiring nothing more than gilding the summer "lily" with my favorite summer liqueur, limoncello.

Cut a small plug out of the watermelon. Pour in the limoncello. Chill the watermelon for 2 hours, or until ready to serve.

To serve, cut the melon into wedges. You may want to have more limoncello on hand for the hardcore folks.

{ BREAKING BREAD: POTLUCKS, COMMUNAL SUPPERS, AND SOIREES }

The Vineyard shows its New England spine in its preferred method of entertaining: the weekend potluck supper. Whether fund-raisers for charities or gatherings of friends, houses from down-island gingerbread cottages to up-island A-frames have tables set with an array of dishes displaying the local bounty.

Private potlucks range from the casual to the elegant, depending on the skills of your friends. The plan is simple: the host house usually arranges for the meat or main dish and the guests bring along their offerings. The truly lost or culinarily inept can usually slide by with a good bottle of wine or a salad. Some of the events get quite competitive, and guests vie for attention with their homemade vegetable creations and fancy desserts.

Public potlucks are even more elaborate. The establishment of a Vineyard convivium (or chapter) of Slow Food, the international culinary organization, was the occasion for a major potluck at the Agricultural Hall. Two tables groaned under the weight of salads made with Whippoorwill or North Tabor Farm greens, of island corn transformed into casseroles, and of locally grown tomatoes topped with snippets of basil fresh from a garden. Wine flowed and the evening ended with a lecture and a taste of classic foodstuffs from the New Orleans convivium.

One of the island's most unusual potlucks is the Soirée Française at the Congregational church in West Tisbury, a monthly gathering of folks who get together to share food and speak French. My mother, who loved the French language and culture, was a regular attendee. One time she dragged me along, complete with my lazy person's offering of a platter of *saucisson sec* and Picholine olives dressed up with a selection of cheeses and some grapes and accompanied by a bottle of red wine that I firmly intended to drink. To my surprise, it was fun! Participants spoke all levels of the language and the most fluent were generous and gracious with those who could barely utter *oui*. I've long threatened to go again. Who knows? I might even cook this time.

Cranberry-Apple Crisp

SERVES 4

Cranberry bogs are to New England what bayous

are to southern Louisiana: a fact of life. The cranberry, called *sassamanesh* by the Wampanoag, is so important that the Wampanoag of Aquinnah celebrate Cranberry Day on the second Tuesday in October. Students are dismissed from school and participate in all kinds of cultural activities. A potluck supper for adults ends the festivities and includes many dishes in which New England's own sweet-tart berry takes center stage. There's sure to be a crisp of some sort on the dessert table.

Preheat the oven to 400°F. Arrange the apple slices and the cranberries in the bottom of a 5-cup baking dish. Drizzle them evenly with the maple syrup and lemon juice. Combine the brown sugar, rolled oats, flour, and butter in a small bowl and mix well. Crumble the mixture evenly over the fruit.

Bake for 15 minutes. Lower the heat to 350°F and continue to bake for 35 to 40 minutes, or until the apples have softened and the topping is golden. Serve bubbling hot topped with the ice cream.

INGREDIENTS

3 Granny Smith apples, halved, cored, and thinly sliced

1 cup fresh cranberries

¼ cup maple syrup

2 teaspoons freshly squeezed lemon juice

¼ cup firmly packed dark brown sugar

½ cup old-fashioned rolled oats

1 tablespoon flour

1 tablespoon unsalted butter, at room temperature

Vanilla ice cream for topping

Sadie Delany's Ambrosia

1 coconut, or 2 cups tightly packed freshly grated coconut and 2 tablespoons coconut water

4 large navel oranges

3 tablespoons superfine sugar, or to taste

Since the book *Having Our Say* became a best seller,

many folks have heard of the centenarian Delany sisters. Sadie, the eldest, was a wonderful cook, and although I never had the pleasure of meeting her, her niece Madelon Delany Stent-Gibel is one of my Oak Bluffs neighbors. We trade recipes and she has always promised me some of Sadie's. I never got one of Sadie's recipes from her, but as fortune would have it, I did end up with one.

I was walking through the Chilmark flea market, where I've spent more than one Saturday morning rummaging through displays in search of antique jewelry, postcards, and other items that I collect. A vendor from whom I'd bought several things in the past rushed up to me with a piece of paper in her hand. On it was a copy of Sadie Delany's handwritten recipe for ambrosia. "I just wanted you to have it," she said. I thanked her and took it home to fiddle with it, as there were no measurements. Like all good old cooks, Sadie Delany relied on the cook to know how to prepare the dish. I've added measurements and now pass it on to you. The number of oranges will depend on the size of your footed compote, so don't be afraid to use a few more.

Preheat the oven to 350°F. Place the coconut in the oven for 15 minutes. As it heats up, it will develop fault lines. Remove the coconut from the oven, then whack at the fault lines with a hammer until the coconut splits open. Strain the liquid inside through a fine-mesh sieve placed over a bowl to remove any pieces of husk. Measure out 2 tablespoons and reserve to use for the ambrosia. (You can drink the rest.) Using a sturdy knife, pry the meat away from the husk and then peel away the brown skin. Grate enough meat to yield 2 cups tightly packed.

Peel the oranges, removing all of the white pith. Slice them crosswise into ¼-inch-thick slices, capturing the juice. Reserve 2 tablespoons of the juice for the ambrosia.

Arrange a layer of the orange slices, overlapping them slightly, in the bottom of a footed glass compote. Top the oranges with a sprinkling of sugar and a layer of grated coconut. Continue layering until the compote is three-fourths full, ending with a layer of coconut. Mix together the reserved 2 tablespoons orange juice and 2 tablespoons coconut water in a small cup, and pour the mixture evenly over the ambrosia. Cover the dish with plastic wrap and refrigerate overnight.

The next day, serve the ambrosia lightly chilled.

Blueberry Crepes

SERVES 6 TO 8

Crepes always look like they take so much trouble

to make, but they really are quite easy and only require a mastery of the batter-swirling technique to achieve professional-looking results. These crepes can be served immediately with a dusting of sugar, or stuffed with whipped cream and blueberries. If you have left-over crepes, they can be tightly wrapped and stored in the freezer for several weeks.

Combine the milk, water, whole egg, and egg yolks in a large bowl and beat with a wire whisk until combined. Gradually add the flour, continuing to beat until you have a smooth batter. Add 6 tablespoons of the butter, the sugar, lemon zest, and vanilla and mix well. Cover the bowl with plastic wrap and refrigerate for 12 hours.

When you're ready to make the crepes, remove the bowl from the refrigerator and allow the batter to come to room temperature. If the batter has separated, stir it gently to recombine.

Place a nonstick 8-inch skillet or well-seasoned crepe pan over high heat until it is hot. It is ready when a drop of water flicked onto the surface sizzles immediately. Lightly brush the pan with a small amount of the remaining 2 tablespoons melted butter. Spoon about 3 1/2 tablespoons of the batter into the skillet and immediately swirl the pan so that the batter thinly and evenly coats the entire bottom. Allow the crepe to cook for a minute or two, or until the edges begin to brown and set. Lift up an edge and flip the crepe. Cook for about 30 seconds on the second side, or until set, and then flip the crepe out onto a baking sheet or plate and let cool. Repeat with the remaining batter, brushing the pan with more butter as needed. Once the crepes have cooled, you can stack them, separating them with sheets of waxed paper, until you are ready to serve them. You should have about 20 crepes.

To serve, place about 2 teaspoons blueberry jam in the center of each crepe and then fold the crepe into quarters. Arrange the folded crepes on a platter and dust the top with powdered sugar and sprinkle with the blueberries. Serve at once.

INGREDIENTS

1½ cups milk

1½ cups water

1 whole egg

2 egg yolks

1½ cups flour

½ cup (1 stick) unsalted butter, melted and cooled

1 tablespoon sugar

⅛ teaspoon freshly grated lemon zest

½ teaspoon vanilla extract

1 jar (8 ounces) New Lane Sundries wild blueberry jam (see Sources, page 198) or your favorite blueberry jam

2 tablespoons powdered sugar

½ cup blueberries

Grand Marnier–Marinated Strawberries *with* Lavender

2 pints strawberries, hulled

¼ cup plus 2 tablespoons Grand Marnier

1 cup heavy cream

1 tablespoon superfine sugar, or to taste

1 teaspoon dried lavender buds

While blueberries are the wild fruit of the island,

there are strawberries in my garden, and some of my friends grow them in window boxes. Sweet, deep red, and overflowing with juice, they are superb for summer eating. I like to doll them up for a more formal dinner by marinating them in Grand Marnier. The orange-flavored spirit, which adds a hint of sophistication, and the topping of whipped cream and lavender buds combine for a perfect ending to a summer Sunday meal.

Slice the strawberries in half lengthwise and place them in a glass bowl. Pour ¼ cup of the Grand Marnier over the berries, cover with plastic wrap, and refrigerate for 2 hours.

When ready to serve, stir the berries and Grand Marnier. Place the cream and 1 table-spoon sugar in a bowl and beat with an electric mixer until the cream begins to thicken. Drizzle in the remaining 2 tablespoons Grand Marnier and continue to whip until stiff but smooth peaks form, adding more sugar if you prefer a sweeter cream.

Spoon a dollop of the cream on top of the berry bowl and dot the cream with the lavender buds. Place the rest of the whipped cream in a small serving bowl. Serve the berries and the cream immediately.

The social ways of Oak Bluffs are a conundrum for those from other parts of the island. Many of us have Southern roots and our inbred sense of etiquette makes us seem to be more formal. Many of us also revel in our summer finery or newly acquired clothing from C'est La Vie or Vital Signs. We eschew the frayed jeans and Birkenstocks or khakis, madras, and Top-Siders that prevail on much of the rest of the island. We also party heartier and relax with the abandon of those who are not always at peace in the world. In Oak Bluffs, folks who spend the year laboring for The Man find solace in a few snatched weeks of comfort among similar folks, where laughter is always long and heartfelt, with heads thrown back and hands slapping thighs.

Nowhere is this more evident than at a five-to-seven, Oak Bluffs's favorite type of party. A five-to-seven is an early-evening house party at which generations mix. When these gatherings began decades ago, refreshments ran to cheese and crackers and pretzels and chips along with mixed drinks. Now, the fare can range from such traditional African American favorites as baked ham with coleslaw and potato salad, or fried chicken with macaroni and cheese, to island delights like smoked bluefish spread, fresh corn, and quahogs—stuffed, fried, or freshly shucked.

Folks on the five-to-seven circuit keep a folding chair or two packed in the trunk of the car so that they're ready to take off on the round of parties that lasts from the Fourth of July until Labor Day. All it takes is a change of clothes from beachwear to elegant summer casual and voilà, party time. Chairs are set up in conversational groups, paper plates are piled high from the groaning boards of delicacies offered by the hosts, and news of recent arrivals and memories of those departed are shared by summer residents and their guests. Five-to-sevens are parties that fulfill the need to be totally at home—what the French call *être bien dans sa peau* (to be at ease in one's skin)—to be able to revel in the company of your peers and breathe deeply of the air of contentment.

{ THIMBLE FARM: PICK YOUR OWN }

One of my favorite pictures of my mother is of her standing in the middle of a field in one of the Hawaiian shirts that she loved to wear in the summers. She's got on an old, beat-up straw hat, and she's clutching a basket half filled with strawberries and grinning like a little girl. I remember the day well.

The bright red strawberry sign on the Edgartown–Vineyard Haven Road had been hanging for years when my mother and I decided to venture down the dirt path to see what lay beyond. There, after a few startlingly deep ruts, we found ourselves at the entrance to Thimble Farm, a pick-your-own strawberry and raspberry farm. We had known the name because Thimble Farm's hydroponic tomatoes arrived in the market in early summer and it was hard to miss their advertisement below the fold of the *Vineyard Gazette*.

For a born New Yorker with an urban New Jersey mom, pick-your-own strawberries were heady stuff. First there were the farm baskets, and then the bending and discovering of the ripe berries under the leaves, and trying not to eat more than I put in the basket. It was even more difficult to pick the ripe raspberries from their thorny bushes without squeezing them into a pulp. We persevered and always managed to get enough to fill up a basket or two. Over the years, we became friendly with the Moskows, the owners of the farm, and we would trade recipes and tales of winter doings with them each summer. A Thimble Farm day became a summer event, and sometimes there was more than one.

I haven't been back to Thimble Farm in years. The Moskows sold it and somehow it slipped my mind until I was searching for some ingredients for a meal, missed the Norton Farm Stand, and got my friend to turn into the Thimble Farm entrance to see what might be available. Now called Benson's Thimble Farm, the place has been transformed into a cut-your-own flower farm, but still sells a few veggies and wonderful tomatoes. As we drove up, Brazilian workers were cleaning carrots, and some tomatoes were available as well. I smiled and watched my past pass by as a car drove up and a mother and daughter got out and headed into the fields to enjoy a late Vineyard afternoon picking flowers and enjoying each other's company.

Gingerbread *with* Blueberries
and Molasses Cream

SERVES 6 TO 9

This gingerbread recipe is a nod to the carpenter

gothic houses that dot Oak Bluffs's historic districts. I live in one such gingerbread house and always like the irony of making a hot-water gingerbread dessert to finish off a formal meal. The topping of molasses-infused whipped cream and blueberries is optional but makes for a fancier dessert.

Preheat the oven to 350°F. Butter an 8-inch square baking pan.

Pour the molasses into a medium-sized heatproof bowl and add the boiling water. Combine the flour, baking soda, cinnamon, ginger, and salt in a sifter or fine-mesh sieve and sift the flour mixture into the molasses mixture. Add the butter and brown sugar and beat well with an electric mixer until smooth. Pour the batter into the prepared pan.

Bake for 35 minutes, or until a toothpick inserted into the center comes out clean. Remove from the oven and let cool on a wire rack for about 10 minutes.

If you wish to serve the gingerbread with the molasses cream and blueberries, place the cream in a bowl and whip with the electric mixer until it begins to thicken. Drizzle in the molasses and continue to whip until stiff but smooth peaks form. The mixture will be a khaki color.

Cut the gingerbread into squares and place on individual plates. Spoon a dollop of the molasses cream onto each serving and then top with the blueberries. Pass the remaining molasses cream at the table for guests to add if they wish.

INGREDIENTS

1 cup dark molasses

½ cup boiling water

2¼ cups flour

1 teaspoon baking soda

½ teaspoon ground cinnamon

1½ teaspoons ground ginger

½ teaspoon salt

4 tablespoons unsalted butter, melted

¼ cup firmly packed dark brown sugar

TOPPING (OPTIONAL)

1 cup heavy cream

3 tablespoons dark molasses

2 cups blueberries

Molasses Cookies

½ cup (1 stick) unsalted butter

1 cup plus 2 tablespoons sugar

1 cup dark molasses

½ cup water

4 cups flour

1½ teaspoons salt

1 teaspoon baking soda

1½ teaspoons ground ginger

¼ teaspoon ground cloves

¼ teaspoon freshly grated nutmeg

¼ teaspoon ground allspice

These cookies are similar to the legendary Joe

Froggers that were originally made in Marblehead, Massachusetts, by a woman named Lucretia, the wife of an African American tavern owner known as Black Joe. If packed in an airtight tin, they reputedly can withstand all sorts of inclement weather at sea, remaining edible. I can't vouch for that claim, as I've never had any last that long in my kitchen.

Combine the butter and 1 cup of the sugar in a large bowl. Using an electric mixer or a wooden spoon, beat together until creamy. Add the molasses and water and stir with the spoon until well mixed. In a separate bowl, combine the flour, salt, baking soda, and all of the spices and stir to mix. Add the flour mixture to the molasses mixture and stir just until you have a smooth dough. Wrap the dough in waxed paper and refrigerate overnight.

When you are ready to bake, preheat the oven to 375°F. Liberally butter 2 cookie sheets. On a floured work surface, roll out the dough ¼ inch thick. Cut out the cookies with a 4-inch round cookie cutter. Arrange the cutouts on the prepared cookie sheets and sprinkle with the remaining 2 tablespoons sugar.

Place 1 sheet in the oven and bake for 10 to 12 minutes, or until golden. Remove from the oven and transfer the cookies to a wire rack to cool. Bake and cool the second sheet of cookies the same way. The cooled cookies can be stacked and stored in an airtight container at room temperature. They will keep for a month or more, if they last that long.

Pegi's Cranberry-Nut Bread

MAKES 2 LOAVES

The McCarthy family have been our neighbors on

the Vineyard for more than forty years. As an only child, I admired the large family of rambunctious children. Pegi was the eldest and over the years we watched as she married and had children of her own. Then, suddenly, Pegi was gone, carried away by an illness. We grieved with the family and watched as her husband raised the children. Now, Pegi's son is one of my neighbors and has a son of his own. I was especially gratified when family matriarch Mabel McCarthy was willing to share Pegi's recipe for cranberry-nut bread.

Preheat the oven to 350°F. Butter two 8 1/2-by-4 1/2-inch loaf pans.

Combine the flour, baking powder, baking soda, sugar, and salt in a large bowl and stir to mix. Add the orange juice, eggs, and butter to the flour mixture and stir to mix well. Fold in the nuts and cranberries. Spoon the batter into the prepared loaf pans, dividing it evenly and making the corners and sides higher than the center. The pans should be three-fourths full.

Bake for 1 hour, or until a toothpick inserted into the center comes out clean. Remove from the oven and let cool slightly in the pans on wire racks, then turn the breads out onto the racks. Serve warm or at room temperature. If you serve only 1 loaf, wrap the second loaf in plastic wrap and refrigerate for up to 1 week.

INGREDIENTS

4 cups flour

2 teaspoons baking powder

1 teaspoon baking soda

2 cups sugar

2 teaspoons salt

1½ cups freshly squeezed orange juice

2 eggs, well beaten

½ cup (1 stick) unsalted butter, melted and cooled

1 cup chopped walnuts

4 cups fresh or frozen cranberries

Mrs. Leonard's Portuguese
Sweet Bread

1½ cups milk

3 packages active dry yeast

1 cup sugar

1 cup (2 sticks) unsalted butter

1 teaspoon salt

8 cups flour

4 eggs

2 teaspoons water

Simply put, Margaret Leonard is my oldest friend

on the island. We met when we were both nine and crawling under the fence to bat tennis balls across a net. I've been lucky to have Margaret as a friend all of these years. She's kept me in touch with the island, giving me some of the inside scoop on the lives of year-round residents and, most recently, her mother's recipe for Portuguese sweet bread. She included this reminder: "This is a real island recipe. The only thing my mom didn't do was put an egg in the middle, which is something that was in the loaves when we got them as holiday gifts." Then Margaret added, "My mom only made this during the winter months. When we came home for lunch and saw bread rising on the radiators, we would race home for a snack after school."

What Margaret didn't say is that Portuguese sweet bread also makes wonderful French toast.

Heat the milk in a small saucepan over low heat until barely warm. Measure out 1 cup into a small bowl and add the yeast and 1 tablespoon of the sugar; set aside. Add the butter to the ½ cup milk remaining in the pan and warm over low heat until the butter melts, then remove from the heat.

Combine the remaining sugar, the salt, and 2 cups of the flour in a large bowl. Using a mixer fitted with the dough hook at low speed or a wooden spoon, beat the milk-and-butter mixture into the flour mixture until blended. Increase the speed to medium (or continue beating by hand) and beat for 2 minutes, or until smooth. Add 3 of the eggs, 2 more cups of the flour, and the yeast mixture and continue beating for an additional 2 minutes. Then slowly beat in just enough of the remaining 4 cups flour to make a soft dough; you may not need all of the flour.

Place the dough on a floured work surface and knead for 10 minutes, or until smooth and silky. Shape the dough into a ball and place it in a large bowl. Cover the bowl with plastic wrap and let the dough rise in a warm spot for about 1 hour, or until doubled in volume.

Butter two 8½-by-4½-inch loaf pans. Punch down the dough, turn it out onto a floured surface, and cut it in half. Cover the dough with a bowl and let it sit for 15 minutes, then remove it, shape it into 2 loaves to fit the prepared pans, and place in the pans. Cover the pans with a clean kitchen towel and allow the dough to rise again in a warm spot for 1 hour, or until nearly doubled.

When you're ready to bake, preheat the oven to 350°F. Beat together the remaining egg and the water in a small bowl. Brush the tops of the loaves with the egg wash.

Bake for 35 minutes, or until the tops are deep brown. Remove from the oven and turn the loaves out onto wire racks to cool. Serve warm or at room temperature. If you serve only 1 loaf, wrap the second loaf in plastic wrap and store in the freezer for up to 1 month.

{ FUDGE WARS }

I have a secret sweet tooth. I can go for months without craving a piece of chocolate, but let me loose in a shop that sells homemade candies and I'm a goner. When I first came to the island, there was only one candy store in Oak Bluffs. Its fire-engine-red sign with tall gilt letters proclaimed DARLING'S, and it was an old-fashioned candy emporium complete with a taffy-pulling machine in the window. I have even found it pictured on the early-twentieth-century postcards of the area that I collect. Saltwater-taffy boxes still bear the name like a whisper from the past.

Darling's, on Circuit Avenue, was the place where everyone went for treats. I was particularly fond of a specialty known as molasses puff: a crunchy confection that was like aerated peanut brittle without the nuts. It was an elusive pleasure, as it could only be prepared when the weather was right: not too damp and not too dry. Over the years, I scarfed down pounds of it until the night that Darling's burned down. I vividly remember the squawk of the horn that called the volunteer firemen from their beds, the wail of the fire engines, and the sad faces the next day as we learned that old man Darling had perished in the fire. The sadness had passed by the following summer, and the shop had moved into smaller quarters next to the movie theater. There was still freshly popped popcorn from the copper kettle or the sticky molasses-covered kind, and I could still get my favorite sugared kernels in brown, pink, and white to accompany my movie viewing. The taffy machine was in place, too, but the molasses puff had become a thing of the past.

Then one day, a second shop opened on Circuit Avenue that sold chocolates, fudge, penuche, and a chocolate-covered toffee dusted with crushed almonds, known as butter-crunch. It was called Hilliard's, and I was in heaven. My adolescent days were spent going from library to candy store and back with small paper boxes of fudge as my reading companion of choice.

Darling's and Hilliard's are gone, their place taken in Oak Bluffs by Ben & Bill's and Murdick's. Ben & Bill's is owned by a branch of the Hilliard family, so the recipe for buttercrunch remains the same, and Murdick's has the fudge monopoly on the island, with shops in Oak Bluffs, Vineyard Haven, and Edgartown. I love the rich, creamy taste of Murdick's chocolate fudge. But no nuts, please—I'm a purist.

Somehow, though, the taste of memory trumps everyday reality and I find myself

longing for a tooth-jarring bite of molasses puff or a taste of multicolored popcorn kernels. Then a friend will appear at my door with a box of chocolate-dipped preserved ginger from Chilmark Chocolates up-island, and the future doesn't taste so bad after all.

Beverages

Oak Bluffs

Oak Bluffs is the part of the Vineyard that I call

home and perhaps its liveliest town. In the summer, it's the place where day-trippers who arrive on a Hy-Line ferry or on the *Island Queen* get their first glimpse of the island, as they walk a gauntlet of restaurants along the edge of the harbor on their way to Circuit Avenue.

I have always felt that this spot owes its special summer bustle to its long history as a resort. In 1835, as Wesleyan Grove, the area was the site of the annual Methodist camp meetings. By the 1870s, the revival movement had grown, and Wesleyan Grove, then named Cottage City, had become popular enough that crowds of thirty thousand attended

the Grand Illumination that marked—and still marks—summer's end. The pious, though, were subjected to an increasing number of distractions, including sea bathing, croquet, and, after 1876, rides on the Flying Horses Carousel, the country's oldest continuously operated merry-go-round. The revival tents gradually were transformed into carpenter gothic Victorian cottages with lacy gingerbread trim, and the community moved from sacred to secular.

The Methodist Campground at the center of town recalls the past and is a photographer's delight. Other visitors enjoy more contemporary pleasures: the beaches, including the Inkwell; the shops on Circuit Avenue; and the numerous restaurants, plain and fancy.

Oak Bluffs is also home to one of the country's few summer communities of African Americans, who have been coming to the Vineyard for more than a century. We bring our own style and exuberance to the island, as we sit on our porches and commune with friends. Like generations of visitors and residents alike, we have come to stay and have made Martha's Vineyard our own.

Porch Sitter

Every Sunday for years, as my friends strolled by

after services at Union Chapel or Our Lady Star of the Sea, I greeted them with my sparkling wine. Several years ago, when Brazilian products became available on the island and I could get the passionfruit juice that I adore, the porch sitter was born. I like to make it with pink Bouvet, an inexpensive French sparkler that is also a good mixer.

Fill a chilled champagne flute one-third full with the passionfruit juice. Top off with the sparkling wine. Voilà.

INGREDIENTS

Passionfruit juice

Dry sparkling wine

Watermelon Agua Fresca

1 watermelon; reserve a few small watermelon wedges for garnish

4 quarts (16 cups) water

1 cup sugar, or to taste

¼ cup freshly squeezed lime juice

The watermelon is totemic to many African

Americans and some of us aren't sure whether to love it or hate it. For a long time, I could take it or leave it, only suffering through the melon so that I could get the rind to pickle (page 70). Suddenly, though, I've found myself craving the stuff and even eating it in the dead of winter. In the summertime, I revel in its sweetness and thump and prod away with the best of them trying to locate the sweetest one around. When I'm tired of eating it (and in a one-person household, a melon can last w-a-a-a-y too long!), I turn it into this agua fresca and serve it in pretty stemmed glasses to my friends.

The size of the watermelon you'll need will vary depending on its juiciness. Trim away the rind, and remove the seeds from the flesh. Purée the flesh in a blender until you have 8 cups.

Place the watermelon purée, water, 1 cup sugar, and lime juice in a large glass crock. Stir well to mix, taste, and add more sugar if desired. Cover and refrigerate until well chilled, or for up to overnight.

Ladle into chilled tall glasses, garnish with the watermelon wedges, and serve.

Bluffs
Bloody Mary

Bluffs

Bloody Marys are the quintessential brunch drink

in Oak Bluffs. I like mine very spicy, and I like the conceit of a pickled okra pod, celebrating my African American heritage, as garnish.

Combine all of the ingredients except the okra pod in a small pitcher and stir well. Pour into a chilled stemmed glass, leaving the ice cubes in the pitcher. Garnish with the okra pod and serve.

INGREDIENTS

½ cup tomato juice

1 jigger Spicy Vodka
(page 189), or to taste

Juice of ½ lemon

1 teaspoon Worcestershire
sauce

1 teaspoon Tabasco sauce

¼ teaspoon celery salt

Prepared horseradish
to taste

Freshly ground black pepper
to taste

2 ice cubes

1 spicy pickled okra pod

Like the country villages that they once were, each island town boasts a small shop that the locals head to for their daily wants and needs. Some, like Cronig's in Vineyard Haven, have morphed into several branches; others are smaller and hark back to times past. Up-island, Alley's General Store is totemic. Located a few steps away from where Music Street meets South Road in West Tisbury, and hard by the town's New England picture-perfect Congregational church, Alley's bills itself as the island's oldest operated retail business, boasting a history going back to 1858.

Step across the threshold of Alley's and be transported to another time. The modern necessities of life are all there, as in any convenience store, but you'll also find treats, ranging from kites for flying on summer breezes to hardware for fixing a squeaky porch door. Shelves are crammed with everything from kids' toys and small souvenirs to oil lamps, in case of power outages, and suntan lotion, for the beach. There are fresh local fruits and vegetables, for those days when the nearby farmers' market isn't open, and video rentals for rainy evenings at home in front of a late-summer fire. This old-fashioned general store even houses West Tisbury's post office, zip code 02575.

Down-island shops are more utilitarian and don't evoke similar nostalgia. Yet on Circuit Avenue in Oak Bluffs, Reliable Market has been just that—old reliable—for decades. Run by the Pacheco family for several generations, the shop is more than the grocery store that it appears to be at first glance. It has one of the largest sections of Brazilian goods of any shop on the island and also sells most over-the-counter medicines to a town that no longer has a pharmacist. The vegetable section gets better each year (arugula made an appearance a few years back, and occasionally even local greens can be spotted among the shrink-wrapped selections).

Bobby Pacheco, the owner and master butcher, can be found most days in the meat section, where he gladly cuts meat to order and advises about which steaks are best for barbecues. His wife is behind the cold-cuts counter, and for many years his mother was in front on the cash register.

When Mrs. Pacheco, the matriarch, stopped working the register a few years back, she could still be found straightening up the shelves, keeping her hand in the family trade. As I was writing this book, I read in the *Vineyard Gazette* that she had died. An era has passed, but I know that everything is ship-

shape in heaven because Mrs. P is up there in her white cotton gloves tidying up and making sure things run smoothly. At the same time, she knows that her family will keep things reliable down here in Oak Bluffs.

Spicy Vodka

I discovered this trick with vodka in the American

Airlines lounge at the Luis Muñoz Marin International Airport in San Juan, Puerto Rico. There, a beautiful glass jar with a spigot is filled to the top with the mix. I have settled for a portable iced-tea dispenser with a spigot, but I dream of a party with enough folks to enjoy a gallon or two of the stuff. The trick is to have a jar where the beauty of the floating peppers can be seen and where the spigot allows you to serve the vodka as you wish. The bell peppers give the vodka a delicate flavor, while the chiles contribute heat. Serve the vodka with a twist of lemon and a dash of dry vermouth in a spicy martini or use it to make a Bluffs Bloody Mary (page 185).

INGREDIENTS

1 red bell pepper

1 green bell pepper

1 orange bell pepper

2 jalapeño chiles, or to taste

1 habanero chile, or to taste

1 quart (4 cups) vodka

Rinse the peppers and chiles well, pat dry, and arrange in a jar. Pour the vodka over them, cap the jar, and allow the mixture to sit for at least 2 days before serving. The pepper vodka will keep for several months, and the flavor will just get richer (and hotter!).

Lemon Verbena Iced Tea

1 teaspoon dried lemon verbena leaves

1 cup boiling water

Ice cubes

Sugar Syrup (page 194) to taste (optional)

I love lemon verbena. I keep trying to grow it with little success, so I buy pounds of it at herb stores in my favorite cities. I like to add it to Moroccan-style mint tea, but most of all I love it in the summer, instead of iced tea. It has none of the caffeine and a wonderfully lemony flavor. Be sure to get lemon verbena, or *Aloysia triphylla*, and not *Verbena officinalis*, also known as vervain. You will need a tea infuser or tea strainer.

Prepare a strong infusion by placing the lemon verbena leaves in a tea infuser and allowing them to infuse in the boiling water for 5 minutes. (If you don't have a tea infuser, put the loose tea in the boiling water and have ready a tea strainer or fine-mesh sieve for straining the liquid before adding the ice cubes.) Remove the tea infuser, add ice cubes to the boiling water, and let cool to room temperature.

Pour into a tall glass filled with ice cubes and top off with cold water. Sweeten with the syrup, if desired, and serve.

{ LEAVIN'S AND LEFTOVERS }

At the end of each summer vacation comes the moment when I have to clean out the fridge that final time and head over to the homes of my neighbors and friends to hand over the slab of bass that won't fit into the cooler and the half-empty jars of ketchup and mustard and mayonnaise and to remind them to pick the last of the vegetables in the garden. Why is it, they must ask, that the case of wine always fits but mustard never does?

Over the years, my long-suffering year-round neighbors and friends have put up with such end-of-season donations that are not going to make it through the winter and that are too fragile to make the homeward journey. I imagine that on some weekend just after the autumnal chill sends the last of us "gulls" scurrying southward for the winter, somewhere on the island there's a huge potluck where the dishes on the table bear the labels of all of the summer residents who have donated the ingredients.

More recently, I've taken to adding a few bottles of wine to the mix. That way, they'll think more kindly of me as they consume the leftovers and leavings and I head home to dream of another year capped by a summer on the Vineyard.

{ WET TOWNS AND DRY TOWNS }

The ways of the Vineyard are mysterious to the novice, and none of them more so than the liquor laws. Ask any first timer who has just settled in to an up-island bed-and-breakfast and feels like having a nightcap, or has arrived at Sunday brunch hankering for a brisk Bloody Mary to start the meal off right. Whoops! No alcohol!

The island's towns are awash in (or aground on, depending on your point of view) a series of varying blue laws, which mean that liquor can be sold in only two towns on the island: Edgartown and Oak Bluffs. Diners who arrive in one of the eateries in the other towns must bring their own bottles. This makes for an awful lot of toting, and for major sales of wine-carrier bags at local shops. The end result is that when my friends and I eat at any restaurant outside of the two "wet" towns, we always arrive with enough wine to slake an army's thirst. As this is frequently also the case with other regular diners, someone at a nearby table usually shares a spare with a hapless first-timer.

The island's liquor stores do a brisk trade to the towns that have blue laws, and if the order is placed before noon or thereabouts, arrival is guaranteed before the preprandial cravings set in. I'm lucky enough to live in Oak Bluffs, so I can freely order a Red Stripe with my fried scallops at Nancy's, or sip away at a bottle of red from the wine list with my dinner at Sweet Life or The Captain's Table. I also am near enough to be able to drop in on Michael Oliveira, my summer Bacchus at Our Market, who suggests the mellow summer reds I love and ensures that my wine rack is never empty. For those who live in other parts of the island and all newcomers, forewarned is forearmed: be sure to bring your own and commit the number of your favorite liquor store to memory. It could save your life, or at least your dinner.

Sugar Syrup

2 cups water

1 cup sugar

This is a simple and elegant way to sweeten

summer's chilled drinks, in which granulated sugar might not easily dissolve. Offer your guests a small pitcher filled with the syrup for sweetening iced tea, lemonade, or any other cool beverage to taste. You can also prepare a sweet syrup in the same way with Splenda for dieting or diabetic friends.

Combine the water and sugar in a 3-quart saucepan and place over low heat. Cook, stirring occasionally, for 5 minutes, or until the sugar has dissolved and the liquid is clear. Raise the heat to medium, bring to a boil, and boil for 1 minute.

Remove from the heat and let cool. Pour into a sterilized jar with a tight-fitting lid and store in the refrigerator. The syrup will keep for several weeks, if it lasts that long in a summer house.

Lavender Syrup

I have tried growing summer roses and the

hydrangeas that are emblematic of the region, to no avail. One summer, though, I discovered that lavender loved the sandy soil that is the lot of many Martha's Vineyard gardeners. Now, I'm working on a border of lavender and mint (another plant that forgives the sandy soil). Not only do I have a flourishing border, but I also have enough lavender to make sachets, lavender bottles to tuck in drawers, and flowers to make the lavender syrup that I use to sweeten lemonade.

Combine the water and the lavender flowers in a 3-quart saucepan and place over medium heat. Bring to a boil, lower the heat to a simmer, and simmer for 3 to 5 minutes, or until very fragrant. Remove from the heat and let steep for 5 minutes.

Strain the liquid through a fine-mesh sieve into a bowl, pressing down on the lavender buds to make sure that all of the liquid is released. Return the liquid to the saucepan, add the sugar, and place over low heat. Cook, stirring occasionally, for 5 minutes, or until the sugar has dissolved and the liquid is clear. Raise the heat to medium, bring the syrup to a boil, and remove from the heat. Let cool, then decant into sterilized bottles. (I use the stoppered bottles that French lemonade comes in, removing their labels first.)

The syrup will keep in the refrigerator for several weeks. Use it to sweeten lemonade, or use it as the base for a cooling drink, adding club soda or plain tap water.

Lemon-Limeade

Ice cubes

2 tablespoons freshly
squeezed lemon juice

2 tablespoons freshly
squeezed lime juice

Sugar Syrup (page 194) or
Lavender Syrup (page 195)
to taste

Thin lime slice and thin
lemon slice for garnish

At the farmers' market in West Tisbury and at the

flea market in Chilmark, the island's favorite tipple seems to be a summery mix of lemon and lime juice flavored with sugar syrup.

Fill a chilled tall glass with ice cubes and add the lemon and lime juices. Top off with cold water and add the syrup until the sweetness suits you. Garnish with the citrus slices and serve.

Boa Noite

SERVES 1

This simple mixture is guaranteed to put you to

sleep with a smile, hence the name, which means "good night" in Portuguese. I came up with it one evening when returning from an island concert with neighbors Ron Gibel and Madelon Delany Stent-Gibel. We all just wanted to relax and have one last drink before evening's end.

Place the ice cubes and rum in a highball glass and top off with the passionfruit juice. The slightly tart taste of the passionfruit perfectly complements the rum—a great way to end any evening.

INGREDIENTS

3 ice cubes

1 jigger dark Barbados rum, or to taste

Passionfruit juice

{ SOURCES }

Chocolate
Chilmark Chocolates
508-645-3013

Hot sauce
Mr. G's Specialties
508-627-4131

Island seafood
The Net Result
508-693-6071
800-394-6071
www.mvseafood.com

Lavender
Spice Barn
614-430-9750
866-670-9040
www.spicebarn.com

Linguiça and *chouriço*
Amaral's Sausage Company
508-993-7645
www.amarals.com

Gaspar's Sausage Company
800-542-2038
www.gasparssausage.com

New England frankfurter rolls
Maple and More
603-878-2525
www.mapleandmore.com

Preserved malagueta chiles
Brazilian Shop
310-837-4299
www.brazilianshop.com

Whole-grain grits
Hoppin' John's
800-828-4412
www.hoppinjohns.com

Wild blueberry jam
New Lane Sundries
508-693-9561

{ ACKNOWLEDGMENTS }

No cookbook is a work of individual effort, so abundant thanks must go to my friends, Fritz Blank and his sous chef Yvette Knight, Priscilla Martel, Barbara Peckham, and Ken Smith, who tasted, tested, and advised. Thanks and bouquets of wildflowers also go to David Amaral, Ali Berlow, "Aunt Vivian" Douglas, Trish and Tony Garnier, Charlayne Hunter-Gault and Ron Gault, Martha Mae Jones, Marvin Jones, Mabel McCarthy, the Larsen family, Margaret Leonard Burke and family, Holly Nadler, Mitzi Pratt, Madelon Delany Stent-Gibel and family, Suesan Stovall, Kate Taylor, Olive Tomlinson, Gretchen Tucker-Underwood, Robin and Ruth Bolles, Keren Tonnensen, Michael Oliveira, Alice Coutinho, Abby Hirsh, Mary Len Costa and family, Gail and Birch McDonough, Kerry Moody, and Cheikh Oumar Thiam. I also thank Abby and Patty at Tuckernuck Antiques, Ron and Paula at Craftworks, Jennifer and Roger at C'est la Vie, and Val at Abode, who allowed me to trade on friendship and graciously loaned items for the photo shoot. Finally, thanks go to my NOLA crews who read and commented; to the one whom I inadvertently forgot; and to all of my friends, named and unnamed, who offered recipes, loaned objects for the photo shoot, hauled me to supermarkets, farm stands, flea markets, and then showed up for dinner.

Special mention must be made of Susie Cushner and her team—Helen Crowther, Jee Levin, and their assistants David and Amy—who schooled me in the ways of food photography and taught me lessons I'll never forget, and to Fan and Don Ogilvie, who kindly loaned their home for the food shots on a rainy week when I was in despair about water coming into my other beloved spot, New Orleans.

No work would ever get off my printer if it were not for my agent Susan Ginsburg and her able assistant Emily Saldino. Finally, thanks must go to Bill LeBlond, Amy Treadwell, Doug Ogan, Evan Hulka, Sharon Silva, Brooke Johnson, and Yolanda Accinelli at Chronicle Books, and Gary Tooth at Empire Design, who saw my Vineyard, knew it well, understood it, and brought it to life.

Index

Table of Equivalents

The exact equivalents in the following tables have been rounded for convenience.

LIQUID/DRY MEASURES

U.S.	Metric
¼ teaspoon	1.25 milliliters
½ teaspoon	2.5 milliliters
1 teaspoon	5 milliliters
1 tablespoon (3 teaspoons)	15 milliliters
1 fluid ounce (2 tablespoons)	30 milliliters
¼ cup	60 milliliters
⅓ cup	80 milliliters
½ cup	120 milliliters
1 cup	240 milliliters
1 pint (2 cups)	480 milliliters
1 quart (4 cups; 32 ounces)	960 milliliters
1 gallon (4 quarts)	3.84 liters
1 ounce (by weight)	28 grams
1 pound	448 grams
2.2 pounds	1 kilogram

OVEN TEMPERATURES

Fahrenheit	Celsius	Gas
250	120	½
275	140	1
300	150	2
325	160	3
350	180	4
375	190	5
400	200	6
425	220	7
450	230	8
475	240	9
500	260	10

LENGTHS

U.S.	Metric
⅛ inch	3 millimeters
¼ inch	6 millimeters
½ inch	12 millimeters
1 inch	2.5 centimeters